5-MIN DAILY

GRATITUDE JOURNAL

PURPOSE GUIDE

POSITIVITY DIARY

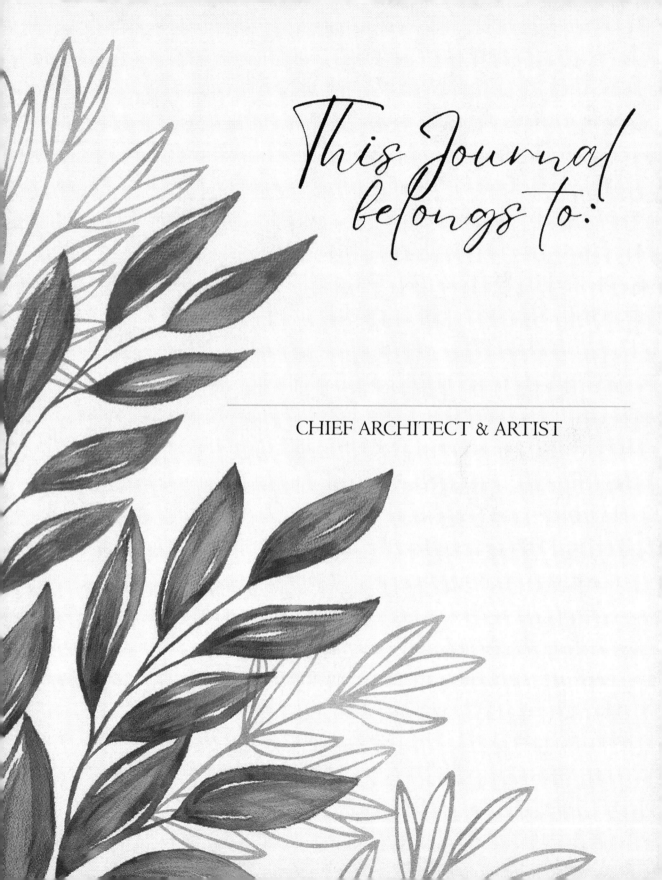

This Journal belongs to:

CHIEF ARCHITECT & ARTIST

SELF–AFFRIMATIONS ARE POWERFUL.

THE NARRATIVE YOU TELL YOURSELF,
— ABOUT YOURSELF, MATTERS.

#YOUMATTER

I am the artist of my life.

The perfect moment is — now.

BEGIN EACH DAY WITH
A SEED OF AFFIRMATION.

Dedication

❧

$\mathcal{D}$edicated to all of the street children in the world.

"*Be* the inspiration."

— Hassan Akmal

Praise for *The Interior Design of Your Career and Life*™

"Akmal's book counsels you on how to navigate with your GPS of passion, towards a meaningful life. To see with your heart and focus on your life's purpose. He demonstrates how to navigate past the meaningless to what really matters: Love, purpose, and the art of living."

— *Alan St. George, master sculptor; president/founder/CEO at Facemakers, Inc. and TitanticClock.com; co-creator and owner, Havencrest Castle*

"Empowering individuals to design their careers and lives is clearly Hassan Akmal's superpower. He does it with charisma, laser-sharp focus, and creativity. His book is original, relatable, profound, poignant, and practical. A treasure of a journey awaits readers who desire to make a difference in their "interior design" life collection — one that will impact the world positively and perpetually."

— *M. Jean-Louis, world-renowned interior designer and principal architect*

"Hassan Akmal has a rare gift in his ability to transform a blurry career and life vision to one that is crystal clear. He frees you from limiting beliefs and teaches you to be the chief architect of your future. His genuine care for, and investment in, others' success come through on every page. Grab a comfortable chair and start writing your story. Your life is about to change."

— *M'Chelle Ryan, director, Upwork Academy*

"While many of us are caught up in the habit of thinking about the next job we want, if we want a truly fulfilling life, we should be thinking about what kind of life we want instead. Hassan Akmal encourages you to take control of your destiny and discover a new way to look at life and a clear approach to unearth new opportunities that maybe were not possible. You will learn how to use your own Kantian life lenses to create value versus focusing on just a positive mindset where you look for the value in what the world is offering you."

— *Francesca Lazzeri, PhD, AI & machine learning scientist, Microsoft*

"This resonant journal, guide, and diary provide a rich, timeless, invaluable, and engaging experience where learning takes place — in the mind, heart, and soul. It challenges our conventional wisdom on career and life coaching from a mastery perspective while providing a real prospect of enduring and tangible benefits. Hassan's inclusion of the sound design framework will resonate with readers as they reflect on their careers and life. In film, sound design is strategically used by the filmmaker to create a unique audio experience that supports the narrative and enriches the story. In applying these tools to their own career and life design, readers will rethink the sound design of their lives while carving out a new space for themselves to reimagine their journey."

— *Tod Oliviere, musician, consultant, and director, student employment and career development, University of California, San Diego*

"This book combines wisdom with the career and life practicalities of tomorrow. The Interior Design of Your Career and Life™ is an invaluable glimmer of hope for those looking to design the rest of their lives. Akmal delivers an enticing call to action to self-design and reconnect with your deeper purpose. His message will intrigue readers to look within to improve and reach their full potential."

— *Greg Costanzo, customer success manager, hiring, LinkedIn*

The Times Square Ball: Image generated with Midjourney

"Every New Year's Eve, at exactly 11:59 pm, the Times Square Ball descends 141 feet, in 60 seconds— along a specially designed flagpole.

Just like watching the sand of an hourglass slowly trickle down, one second at a time, one grain at a time, New Yorkers and countless tourists from all over the world gaze at the lighted-paneled ball, as if they are looking into the future. And—they are, mesmerized.

Perspectives change over time, just like careers. They evolve, and each year, we evolve.

Since 1920, the ball has gone through a plethora of revisions, eventually becoming the magnificent work of art the world sees now; a crystal ball made up of almost 3000 crystal triangles illuminated by over 30,000 LED lights. In each triangle lives a story of heartbreak and hope, chased away by the lights of a new horizon.

Beneath that resplendent ball, we make our New Year's resolutions and promises to loved ones, but above all—to ourselves. It's where some dreams end, and others begin.

There below (close by), is a magical place, where the manifestations of these New Year's resolutions are realized. Our students and alumni love this place. They can be themselves and aspire to be anything they wish to be. It's called the Career & Life Design Lab. They enter with hopes and dreams, with embers of fear, but leave with aspirations of self-reinvention. The designing of your life.

This a story about being a storyteller with no end date in sight. This is about your story, your True North — the direction of the rest of your life."

— *Hassan Akmal, TEDx Talk, March 27, 2021*

New Year's Eve in Times Square: Image generated with Midjourney.

IN REMEMBRANCE OF
Mohammad Afzal Chaudhry

March 29, 2023

"Indeed, to Allah (God Almighty) we belong, and to Allah, we shall return."

إنا لله وإنا إليه راجعون

Uncle Afzal was a second father to me. He passed away on March 29, 2023,
which is also the 35th anniversary of my father's passing. He was a film director
and belived that film-making is a live mirror into your career and life.

"Sometimes when you are in a dark place,
you think you have been buried,
but actually you have been planted."

—*Christine Caine, Activist, Author, and Founder of Propel Women and*
The A21 Campaign that combats human trafficking around the globe

Connect On Social Media

YouTube Channel: @CareerandLifeMastery

LinkedIn: LinkedIn.com/in/hassanakmal

Facebook: @CareerMastermind

Instagram: @HassanAkmal, @CareerandLifeMastery

Twitter: @LifeMastermind, @MastermindCode

TikTok: @CareerandLifeDesign

Learn more about the Author:
www.HassanAkmal.com

Learn more about Career and Life Mastery:
www.CareerandLifeMastery.com

Resources:
www.CareerandLifeMastery.com/mastery-resources

TEDx Talk: https://youtu.be/SEa14Q-KdwY

The Power to Design a Life You Love:

Five Secrets to Career and Life Mastery

——*And Why Success Is Not Everything*

(Includes a Special Tribute to Kobe Bryant)

For speaking engagements, please email:
CareerandLifeVision@gmail.com

Published in the United States.

Names: Akmal, Hassan, author.

Title: The Interior Design of Your Career and Life ™: 10-Week Gratitude Journal, Purpose Guide, and Positivity Diary

Description: First Edition. | Rancho Santa Fe, California, 2023.

ISBN: 978-1-7335593-0-0 (Paperback)

Subject: Vocational guidance. | self-realiztion. | SELF-HELP / Motivational & Inspirational.

Book Cover and Interior Design by Hassan Akmal

ALSO BY HASSAN AKMAL

How to be a Career Mastermind™: Discover 7 "YOU Matter" Lenses for a Life of Purpose, Impact, and Meaningful Work

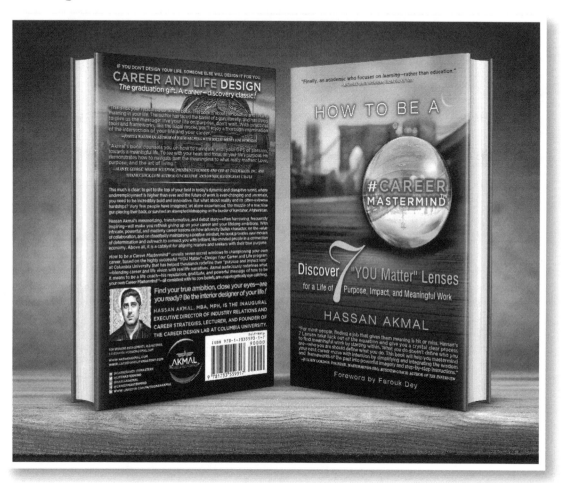

Available in Paperback, Hardcover, eBook, and Audio Book

#CareerMastermind

REMEMBER, THE ART OF BALANCING VISION IS IN OUR DNA—LITERALLY. WE HAVE MAJOR AND MINOR GROOVES IN LIFE, AND THESE PATHS SHOULD BE ALIGNED AND PARALLEL. IF NOT, THEY WILL CLASH OR BE TOO FAR APART, AND THAT WILL HINDER YOUR GROWTH AND PROGRESS."

—HASSAN AKMAL

WWW.CAREERANDLIFEMASTERY.COM

#Mindset   #HassanAkmal   #TEDx   #Purpose

THE INTERIOR
DESIGN
OF YOUR CAREER
AND LIFE™

HASSAN AKMAL

Purpose Series

This symbol represents the Mastermind Agreement and Code defining the journey of the Career Mastermind™. It is inspired by the falcon — a bird gifted with intelligence, speed, and accuracy. It has been associated with visionary power, wisdom, and guardianship — a guide to each individual's life purpose. The letter A evokes the falcon in its appearance of upward flight, like an arrow. It signifies aspiration and the ascent of career and personhood, guided by the Master's strong wings of experience.

#MastermindCode

THE
MASTERMIND
CODE™

FIND
YOUR

CENTER OF
GRAVITY

Sunset: La Jolla Shores, San Diego

"Your vision will become clear only when you can look into your own heart. Who looks outside, dreams; who looks inside, awakes."

—*Carl Jung*

"Thousands of candles can be lighted from a single candle, and the life of the single candle will not be shortened. Happiness never decreases by being shared."

—*Buddha*

CONTENTS

— ◆◆◆ —

PART I: Turning Inward

PART II: Your Canvas

PART III: Designing the Rest of Your Life

This is your theatre of space.

Use your sense of discovery"to find it.
The same vision of space applies in
your career and life. You with me?

Author's Note

Imagine — You Are The Artist of Your Life

An incredibly ambitious game called RoVille is a massively multiplayer version of The Sims, a series of life simulation video games. Players have the ability to build their own businesses and homes in an open universe. There are even automobiles to drive, jobs to hold, and places to explore. The limit is only their imagination.

Kids of any age can create an account on Roblox with no parental restrictions The building interface function allows walls, doors, and windows to be placed anywhere a player sees fit, and the game also allows for them to build multi-story constructs. What's more intriguing is not how many levels or stories one might dream into reality, but the story the player is writing and self-creating as the chief architect.

Success is seeing what others cannot. It is not the exterior design that ultimately matters when it's seen from the outside, nor what others may think. But, how you feel and how your vision is reflected from the heart of the design — from within.

Your story — the story behind the design is *The Interior Design of Your Career and Life*™.

Begin With Humility

Gratitude grounds us. It's both a starting point and an ending point. Beyond this, it's an infinite mindset that helps us focus on abundance vs. scarcity. When uncertainty exists in some areas of our lives, certainty is visible and real in many others. It's a positive emotion that leads to positive thoughts and opportunities.

Bringing the Outside In

Each one of us faces sensory distraction, or how we experience our external world through our senses. This cognitive distraction is a signal to reevaluate our physical environments. Designing for our own cognitive and sensory wellness in environments increases the likelihood of feeling at home in our surroundings. This leads to more satisfaction at home or wherever you live and work.

Many studies make a case for creating a palette of typologies that nourish the senses and promote focus. Spaces need to be designed to meet each person's unique demands by realizing that we all have varying thresholds and tolerances. What's important to you is at the center of each design, each collection.

Life is a journey of experiences. We face hardship and tests in our careers and lives that we don't anticipate. Self-belief, a clear vision, and aligning true purpose exist at the crossroads of adversity and never giving up.

The interior design process examines the acoustic, textural, and visual elements in your career or life. This is beyond the decor, furniture, or lighting selections. It's more than specific typologies that motivate or influence how one might experience a space.

For example, one might embrace highly textured and colorful spaces because they inspire creativity. Another person may prefer a warm fireplace, soft surfaces, or natural colors because they provide a sense of calm.

Metaphorically, the combinations of design elements and what they represent in your career and life affect your behavior over time. For example, perhaps you have a priceless memory in your life that is reflected in a picture in your bedroom. Similarly, you reverse engineer from career and life experiences. They build upon one another and help you create a sense of belonging and purpose.

Let's be clear. The goal here is to design a space for you to think, reflect, and visualize your careers and life first. Once you have this space, you will guard it no matter what it takes. Then, you will have the freedom to design the life you love.

The power of applying human-centered design is that it begins with empathy for your own uniqueness and lifts you up. You must stay focused on your realizing your vision. Even if you are broken, there is always hope. This is not just interior design or construction of a new road, it's self-construction.

Picking Up the Pieces

Kintsugi is the Japanese art of repairing broken pottery by mending the areas of breakage with powdered gold.

Career and life design is much like Kintsugi. We dig deep when life happens, and we become stronger through adversity. We reverse engineer from our pain and we heal wiser. We must embrace our losses and celebrate them, not ignore them. They are a part of us. We should be grateful for them.

Front view of a repaired Kintsugi bowl: Image generated with Midjourney

Happiness doesn't come from a perfect life or from being perfect. All beautiful things have unique imperfections. Your scars, wounds and shortcomings are your beauty. You grow as a designer in life and learn to endure them with grace.

Like broken objects mended with gold — we are all Kintsugi.

The breakage and mending are all honest parts of our past and should be celebrated, not hidden. They are pieces and parts of who you are. In fact, we design from them when it comes to the interior design of our career and life. They inspire us, filling the cracks with hope, and become the inspiration and centerpieces in our career and life design.

My Kintsugi bowl (of life) is the centerpiece of my home. I have another piece — — a Kintsugi (career) vase, that is in the center of my office. They have a whole different set of experiences. But, both of them help me re-center.

Every heart is damaged. Some of your hearts are broken right now. You're all more beautiful — for having been broken.

Your heart is your canvas. See into it and through it.

Don't hide the scars — be your own Kintsugi Master.

—— **Hassan Akmal, MBA, MPH, 3/23/2023**
Executive Director, Career and Professional Development, UC San Diego, Author, Professor, Future of Work Expert, and TEDx Speaker

"Space is where miracles happen."

—*Rich Litvin, co-author of The Prosperous Coach*

Foreword

— ◆ —

*L*ife is one big adventure.

That reality can either excite you or frighten you. Before the Great Recession of 2008-2009 I would have said adventure sounded fun. I was certainly up for one when my wife and I moved 1000 miles away from home to begin a new chapter in Tampa, Florida. But 5 months into our new life in the Sunshine State, and after buying our first house and our first baby, I lost my job. The company I worked for at the time ran out of money and had to let me go.

This was not the kind of adventure I was hoping for.

After burning through our savings I got honest with myself: I didn't want to find another job. I never felt like I belonged in an office, behind a desk, working for someone else. Plenty of people do, but it just wasn't for me. Up until losing my income and going on food stamps (again, not the kind of adventure I imagined) I didn't have the courage to go out on my own and try to start a business. But this dark moment became a unique opportunity for me to be reborn as it were and try something new.

I began to dream again.

What kind of life did I want to live? What kind of work excited me? What kind of people did I want to be around and serve? How many hours or days each week did I want to spend working versus being with my young family? Could I really work from home and not lose my mind?

Hassan's concept of Interior Design for your life is powerful, and back then I was just starting to discover how much say we have over how our lives turn out. It was clear that there were plenty of things out of my control. But at the same time there were just as many that were in my control, and those were the things I focused on.

I committed to creating the most helpful audio content on the internet, teaching musicians how to record music on a budget. Specifically this looked like posting 3 pieces a week (two articles and one YouTube video). I gave as much value for free as I could, figuring I could find a way to monetize it on the backend.

From day one I blocked off every Friday and vowed never to work a Friday again. They became "family fun Fridays" as I would take my wife and daughters to the beach, the zoo, or the pool. Weekends were for family and recovery. Work would have to fit into Monday through Thursday.

I committed to starting my day with prayer and bible reading instead of Facebook or Twitter. And we as a family have always shut things down before dinner time so we can come together around the table (technology free!).

As a trained audio engineer, sound is a big deal to me. I love the sound of trickling water in our swimming pool outback or the sound of ocean waves hitting the shore. Hence, these are two of my happy places and where I go to get inspiration for new content on YouTube, my podcast, or my next book.

Interestingly enough, when we listen to different sounds or music, our mood can change. Feeling sad after a tough conversation or breakup? Listening to upbeat music can literally lift your spirits. Need to calm down after a hectic or stressful day? Turning on some chill LoFi can mellow you out and help you wind down for the evening.

In much the same way the thoughts and beliefs and interior narratives we tell ourselves everyday can not only affect our mood, but the direction of our lives.

In more ways than one, Hassan Akmal is correct - you are the artist of your life.

You can only use what God gave you (your talents, skills, passions, personality, opportunities), but how you use those "colors" or "instruments" will determine the "painting" or "song" you create. You are the one who gets to decide how to apply the raw materials of your life, for better or for worse.

And all of it begins with your mind and what you tell yourself.

After seeing Hassan's TEDx talk I knew he was onto something. This journal will be instrumental in the adventure of your life. If you use it and apply the principles inside, you will view the adventure of life as something to be excited about and not afraid of.

Here's to you creating a life worth living!

Graham Cochrane

Author of How to Get Paid for What You Know: Turning Your Knowledge, Passion, and Experience into an Online Income Stream in Your Spare Time, TEDx speaker, and host of the Graham Cochrane Show podcast

www.GrahamCochrane.com

Graham Cochrane

THE KEY TO MEANING IS PURPOSE

Happiness comes and goes — like money, but meaning and purpose remain. Lift yourself above the hustle and bustle by finding your "flow". Flow is the psychology of optimal experience. For example, it's when you are "in the zone" as a tennis player or athlete. When you are in this state of mind, you lose your sense of time and place, and everything falls like dominos in the right direction. It's when it clicks when the aces happen and the serve "pops," and when you find the sweet spot in your form and energy.

MOMENT BY MOMENT

How can you experience life the way you
want to experience it?

_____

_____

DESIGN YOUR PURPOSE

How does one find or create calling?

_____

_____

LIFE IS WORTH LIVING

Does money define happiness? If yes,
to what extent?

_____

_____

You are unique.
Nobody else is you.

Design Your Purpose

Use all the blank pages with tiles to create your Purpose. Remember, if it's not achievable, it's not your purpose.

Begin with your peaks and valleys.

Peaks:

Write down a situation in your life — whether you were at work, at home, or elsewhere — when you felt completely energized and fulfilled. What were you doing? Who was present? What was going on?

Valleys:

Write down a situation in your life that you really disliked or found demotivating or unsatisfying. When or why did your energy fall?

Preface

Now more than ever, people are voluntarily leaving scripted lives in search of more meaning. According to Upwork, 76 percent described themselves as responsible for driving their own career in 2022. Whether you are career transitioning to a new organization or industry, advancing within the same company, or taking a risk and trying something brand new, it takes courage and conviction. However, creating a career and life vision is no easy task.

For over 15 years I have been coaching individuals to see from the heart and then strive toward their purpose. Life has taught me one critical thing; your vision is a pact with yourself — nobody else.

But, what if I were to tell you that you can create this sanctuary of self-reflection within yourself? That you are in fact, the "interior designer" of your career and life.

Before you can have a vision for your career and life, you have to build the *space* where you will create your purpose. You are designing the space to design. It's a mind-and-heart creative space to build your career and life vision.

Everything is an experience. No detail is too small. It starts with inspiration and you reverse engineer from experiences. Experiences lead to transformations. Transformations lead to stories. Stories lead to actions. Actions lead to fulfillment.

You are your story. You are the artist of your life. The designer of your life.

Design Your Work Space

Imagine the dividing line between work and the rest of your life — happily blurred. You must clear your vision before you can focus your vision.

The phenomenology of how our surroundings affect us and how these spaces become deeply intertwined with our sense of self and our sense of belonging is highly underrated. There are social, functional, aesthetic, and temporal dimensions of the workplace that impact our holistic and immersive experiences. These elements transcend time, are ongoing, and we absorb them unconsciously.

That being said, what if we could intentionally control the environmental psychology? Meaning, that we could control the flow of environment into our our design? Specifically:

Sensory: Our view, maximizing natural lighting, sounds, smells, textures, colors, and what we see when we take a walk around.

Functional: Physical attributes — functionality plus a good design equals a memorable and meaningful experience.

Social: Interpersonal aspects and interactions within the community you choose to live and work in.

Temporal: Inflection points and markers on the progress towards goals and aspirations.

There is untapped potential for improving and making a positive impact on our own well-being through human-centered design. The career and life circles are one of the same. Envision an infinity symbol (∞), they are intertwined. It's an 8, my favorite number, but sideways. The passion transformed into purpose — connected and linked.

The grains of an hour glass represent what we pour into ourselves and how quickly or slowly it impacts us overtime. We must set our own parameters and boundaries.

Work should not compete with life, nor vice-versa. It's not a balancing act. It is about balance but not in the traditional sense, it's about integration and alignment. You may have heard the saying, "What you do doesn't define who you are, you define what you do." This is precisely the point. When you reframe this, your perspective changes (and sharpens), and as a result — your life improves.

You are the film-maker.

Career and Life Vision

Balancing
**Career and
Life Vision**
against the
token of time

Designed by Hassan Akmal

Fall in Love With Your Craft

Fall in love with your craft. Be unapologetic about investing in it.

Design your true path.

Aligning Your Career and Life Prisms with Your "YOU Matter" Lenses (Eyepieces)

Life Bucket List

Career Bucket List

LIFE BUCKET LIST

1. BUY NEW HOUSE
2. ADOPTING A PET
3. PAY OFF LOANS AND CREDIT CARDS
4. MOVE TO A NEW CITY
5. STARTING A FAMILY
6. NEW CAR
7. TRAVEL
8.
9.
10.
11.
12.
13.
14.
15.

CAREER BUCKET LIST

1. PROMOTION
2. PAY RAISE
3. TRANSITION TO NEW CAREER
4. MEETING TARGETS
5. SIDE HUSTLE
6. START OWN COMPANY
7. REBRAND DIGITAL IDENTITY
8.
9.
10.
11.
12.
13.
14.
15.

CAREER

VISION

LIFE

Aligning Your Career and Life Prisms with Your "YOU Matter" Lenses (Eyepieces)

LIFE BUCKET LIST

1 _____
2 _____
3 _____
4 _____
5 _____
6 _____
7 _____
8 _____
9 _____
10 _____
11 _____
12 _____
13 _____
14 _____
15 _____

CAREER BUCKET LIST

1 _____
2 _____
3 _____
4 _____
5 _____
6 _____
7 _____
8 _____
9 _____
10 _____
11 _____
12 _____
13 _____
14 _____
15 _____

CAREER — LIFE

Introduction

The three most powerful words in the English language are ....? They will absolutely change your life; do you know what they are?

Repeat after me, "I DON'T KNOW."

We want to start with openness and a place of curiosity because that's the space and place where learning can take place.

Sometimes we project like we have it all figured out, but we don't. Otherwise, we would already be where we want to be. We also don't want to come to a reflection experience with our minds full. If you do that, there is no room for me, for you — or anyone else to pour anything in.

Glass full and overflowing: Image generated with Midjourney

We don't want to graduate at the end of this journal the same person we were before.

What will it be? A moment of peace or a moment of regret? You decide.

Building a career and life vision has three essential elements:

    1) Clarity (*including over limiting beliefs*)

    2) Focus (*that will lead to focal points and branches to your career and life tree trajectories*)

    3) "In-sight" (*inner-viewing, self-awareness, deep reflection, and true consciousness*)

Clarity is the big picture — the <u>where</u>.

Focus follows and is — the <u>how</u>.

Your internal reflection, prayer, and/or meditation will lead you to — the <u>why</u>.

Start with the Self. We all want more in life. We know there is more out there for us. This is your search for that *more*.

You will use interior design concepts and ideas to help you imagine your life and future. You will also leverage symbolism, and analogies, and metaphors to help you envision your best self in your best life — aligned with your Purpose.

Who is the light in your life? Where do you feel most comfortable? How do you want to impact people and the world? Your self-consciousness and intuition are critical to answering this question. Consider who and what you are taking with you on this journey. The people, the environment, and the materials. This is your journey and design. This guide will serve as your roadmap. Use it to record your career and life bucket lists, what is standing in the way, and how you can overcome those obstacles.

Remember, this guide is both for your career and life, as they go hand-in-hand. Think about what the perfect workday would look like for you. How many hours a week would you want to work? How would the transition from work to life feel each day? Would you relocate?

Some of you will be designing a new space, but others are designing into a space they already are in. The materials and surroundings are evolving. They are like the pixels of a vision you have. You start with a few and you build up, then add and subtract until ultimately you have a full picture. Do not rush this process, build one pixel at a time. Make them count and align them with meaning. The brightest one will be your North Star. Follow it. Experience this journey. Experience this design.

What is Career & Life Design? It's self-awareness and self-design. You are leveling up your skills to be "future-ready" — planting a seed for your perpetual growth. You are building character. This is about your story — the story of the rest of your life. This story has no end and is ever-evolving. You are writing your story to tell your story one day. And as long as you don't stop writing — and don't stop living, your story will become your freedom.

Reverse engineer from the situations that bring out the best in you. Believe in the moments and bring your own magic and patterns into your career and life design. Break the rules. For example, sometimes something doesn't match but it adds character or warmth. It should be a reflection of you and what makes you unique. An experience can be many things. You define them. You can create those special moments that will last forever.

This ten-week journal offers a simple, yet powerful pen-to-paper method to empower you to design multiple careers and your life over a lifetime. Begin by investing just a few minutes a day to think in this space and write. Here you will discover the power of positivity, perspective, and mindset. Don't give up, keep writing. With time you will build clarity and create purpose.

Each morning, begin with 1) meditation and prayer, 2) an affirmation, and then dive into your, 3) interior design collections, your design project — your career and life. Finish each day with, 4) gratitude an reflections. Use interior design concepts and ideas to help you imagine your life and future. Leverage the symbolism, analogies, and metaphors to visualize the path to get you there — with the goal of being a better version of yourself than yesterday.

There are ten weeks, so there are ten collections. Each collection should reflect a different perspective of your vision and calling. This is the art of living.

Will this be a new construction in your life or a renovation or upgrade of what's already there? The decision is yours. You are the chief architect.

Let's begin your journey.

The Interior Design of Your Career and Life

The interior design of your career and life is a creative design space with no borders — a sanctuary of self-reflection. This is your space, nobody else's. And — don't forget that *you* are a part of the design.

You must learn to love and invest in yourself to fully be able to see this masterpiece. We all have a base self and a best self. And sometimes there is friction between those two. We have to retrain ourselves, and let our bodies know who is in control. We have a body and we have a mind, but who is the *real* you or the controlling agent? When not the mind, nor the body, but the heart or (the highest self) is in charge, we gravitate to our best self.

Defining your career and life vision is like excavating gold. First, you need to believe that there is gold in the ground. Some of us have self-doubt. But once you believe, then you start digging.

Think of your mind as a *gold* mind. When you excavate gold, you sift through the dirt, and the gold that is heavier stays on the bottom. The dirt comes out and the gold shines.

You are that gold.

Top view of a repaired Kintsugi bowl: Image generated with Midjourney

CAREER AND LIFE

To be a Career Mastermind™, you must also be a Life Mastermind. Career and Life are parallel to each other, not competing with each other. Your career and life overlap, intersect, and superimpose one another. The goal is to have them mirror one another so they are seen as one. Think of it as a DNA double helix. Their motion is in balance and is the same, although they are different and run in opposite directions.

DNA contains the instructions needed for an organism to develop, survive and reproduce. To carry out these functions, DNA sequences must be converted into messages that can be used to produce proteins, which are the complex molecules that do most of the work in our bodies. A Career Mastermind™ has these instructions, as does a Life Mastermind, and they partner in harmony.

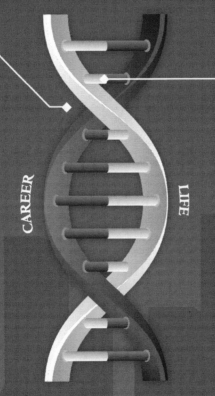

CAREER

LIFE

The horizontal lines you see in the image represent base pairs. They come together by an "H" bond, or "Hassan" bond for the purpose of this book. It's the catalyst that unites these two distinct paths. I's the base and purpose, stabilizing the DNA. These pairs are complementary and interact with each other as our work and life do in our daily lives. It's "in our DNA."

MAJOR GROOVE

MINOR GROOVE

The double helix is right-handed (meaning your life lens leads it) with about 10–10.5 base pairs per turn. Think of these as steps in your career and life. They can be days, weeks, or years, even seconds. They are measured by the intensity and outcome. Each set of 10-01.5 base pairs represents years, or stages in your life. The double helix structure of DNA contains a major groove and minor groove. These represent setbacks and shortcomings. We all have them and they happen to everyone. But, we bounce back, and never lose faith. The major groove occurs where the backbones are far apart, the minor groove occurs where they are close together. The more aligned they are, the better off we are.

Designed by **Hassan Akmal**
Illustration by **Ahmed Zaeem**

Imagine Living Your Purpose

Unlock your career and life vision — by unlocking your imagination.

Your heart can see and feel things the brain cannot. So, lead with it.

PART II

This is
your
canvas.

You are the artist of your life.

"YOU Matter" Purpose Lenses

Many people don't love themselves. This needs to change. Forgive yourself for the past and promise yourself a new future. It's time to see things and yourself differently.

Lenses come in all shapes and sizes. Some are used to concentrate light into a parallel beam so you can see it at a great distance. The lenses of binoculars, however, do the opposite. They focus light rays from far away so you can see distant things more clearly. These are the lenses we are referring to, the ones that help us see our career and life vision more clearly. The way light bends when it travels from air to water or glass is called refraction. Refraction is the key to how lenses work — and lenses are as essential to binoculars as they are for us to see what's far away in our future, closer and more clearly.

The reason the lenses in my previous book, *How to be a Career Mastermind*™: *Discover 7 "YOU Matter" Lenses for a Life of Purpose, Impact, and Meaningful Work*, are called "YOU Matter" Lenses is because each lens belongs to you, nobody else. The teachings of the 7 "YOU Matter" Lenses, each of which is dealt with in chapters 1 — 7 of the book, will help you cultivate the right mindset.

Prisms are heavy. Our life prisms are full of limiting beliefs, and our career prisms are full of extrinsic motivators. These weigh us down and sometimes get misaligned, making our vision blurry. Prisms are larger wedges of glass that rotate images. Without them, light rays that pass through a convex lens from a distance look like they're upside-down. Prisms rectify this issue and help us see correctly — not only in binoculars but in our own sometimes blurred perspectives.

Knowing that we have these prisms, we must also understand that our life and career prisms are in constant conflict with each other, against time. For example, our work/ life balance can be very challenging. The harder and longer you work, the less time you have for yourself or your family, friends, significant others, or pets. On the contrary, the more time you spend on vacation or at home, the less productive you are. Our career and life visions are competing against each other. But should they be?

My goal for you is that you will approach any challenges you face with resilience and insight. Revisit the lenses in their full context in my first book to explore the full scope of each. I am also including them here for your reference so that you can keep them top-of-mind as you begin each week.

Visualize how you will apply each principle in your life. Challenge yourself to build (not find) that purpose, and if you already have it, refine it.

While there are many books on the topic of personal career development, this book takes on a much broader perspective, helping you envision personal goals that have a global impact. Observation, philosophy, discovery, and experience meet in a workbook that helps define ultimate meaning and purpose with *self* as a component of humanity.

We all need a Purpose greater than ourselves.

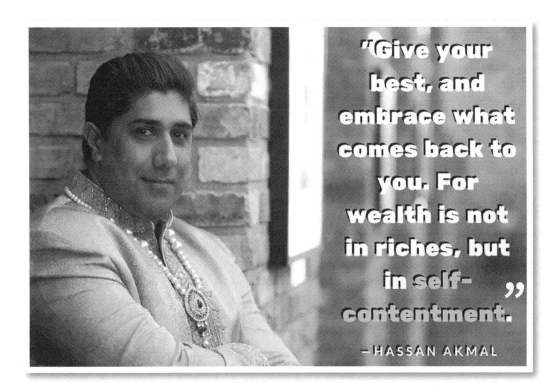

> "Give your best, and embrace what comes back to you. For wealth is not in riches, but in self-contentment."
>
> —HASSAN AKMAL

Lens 1

Positive Mindset — Almost Everything is Perspective

TURN TO CLEAR VISION

If you change your perspective, you can change your life.

Lens 2

The Unlock: Career and Life Vision

Clarity of your vision is central to your ability to visualize your path and definition of success.

Lens 3

Discovery Calls — The Purpose in You

Your Purpose is within you but is greater than you.

Lens 4

Career Manifestó: Be an Architect, Build the Life You Love

Your manifestó is yours, which means intentionality and being true to yourself.

Lens 5

"YOU Matter" — Why You Should Invest in Yourself

Self-care is different from self-love. You must sincerely believe that you deserve more.

Lens 6

Your Own Personal Business Plan

You must be the chief executive officer of your own career and life.

Lens 7

A Noble Career and Moral Compass

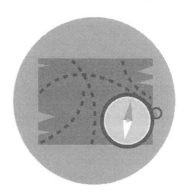

Your core values will align with your Purpose.

"YOU MUST LIVE IN YOUR PURPOSE.

Like with binoculars, collimation is the alignment of all optical elements along the binocular axis. This is what you are doing with your life. You are aligning your lenses. You are combining your paths in your quest for happiness."

—Hassan Akmal

www.CareerandLifeMastery.com

#CareerMastermind

Your Life's Blueprint

Begin outlining ideas for your career and life design blueprint. Here are four steps to help you get started before you begin the 10-Week deep dive into your interior design.

1) Start with an imaginative walkaround of the place or property you visualize living in one day. However, instead of a property or a house, it could also be your zenith or final destination in terms of where you want to be in your career and life vision. It can even be a feeling that speaks to the big picture. You will dive into the architecture, lighting, and colors in much more detail with each collection, so keep it light for now — the goal here is just to get started.

2) Go room by room: Draw walls first. The first room might be a master bedroom or a safe space, something private, or where you can feel secure. Perhaps you want to start with the kitchen or food? Think about what makes you feel alive. Perhaps it's a ranch with horses like my blueprint has.

3) Next: Add doors, windows, and stairs. What are some new doors or opportunities you need in your career or life? What windows will you need and how transparent and large do they need to be? What do they symbolize and represent in terms of your career and life? Is there are role in your career that you feel is unreachable? If so, build a new staircase that leads to it. Will it be a spiral staircase? How many levels? Small steps or large steps, you decide.

4) Add fixed installations. These are things you may not be able to change in your life or things that you are not willing to settle on. Make sure you explore all of the dimensions and layers. Move on to the next room after completing one section.

Remember, a blueprint is a duplicate of a technical drawing. It empowers you to visualize a more extensive project from a picture, and it simplifies the process to ensure that all steps are taken when building the project. With this step-by-step guide, you'll better understand how to make a blueprint for your own career and life project.

Career and Life Design Blueprint

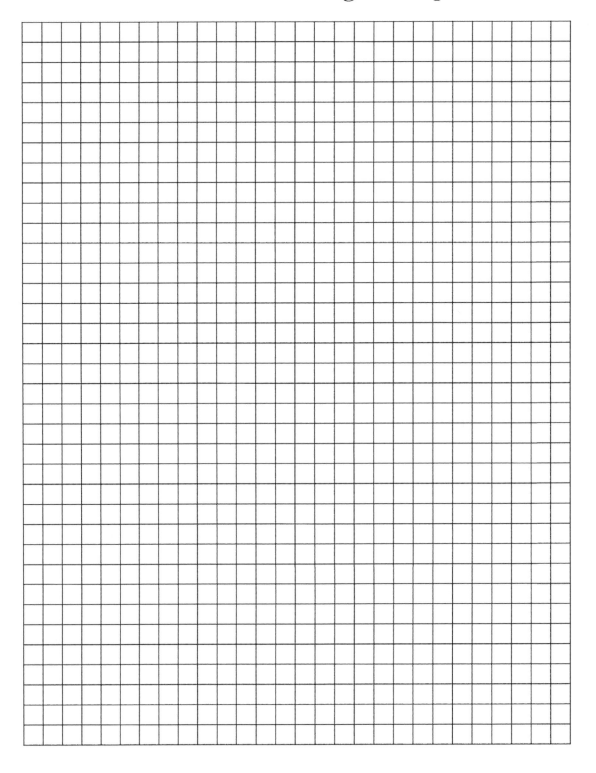

Career and Life Design Blueprint

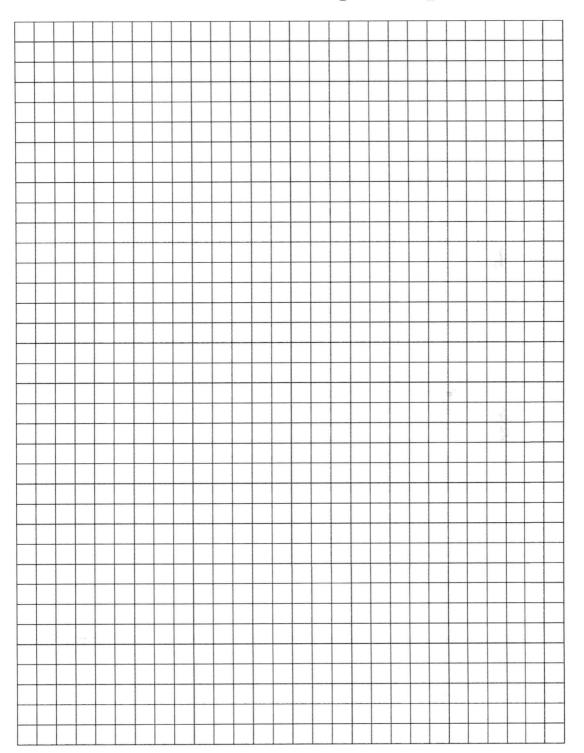

CALIBRATING YOUR CAREER AND LIFE VISION IS LIKE CALIBRATING BINOCULARS

The diopter adjustment is a control knob on your binoculars. It is designed to let you compensate for differences between your own two eyes.
Once you set the diopter, then the two barrels should stay in proper relation. From then on you can focus, just by turning the central focusing knob.

Close your eyes, clear your mind, now open them.

CAREER VISION
Create a career bucket list in your imagination, what would it look like if time or money wasn't an issue? Where would you be working? What would you be doing and why?

LIFE VISION
Imagine your life in the far future, as clearly as you would visualize the rest of your day today or the week ahead. How much time would you have after work for yourself or family?

Turn off your racing thoughts. Take a deep breath. "Reset"

TURN TO CLEAN VISION

QUARTERS ONLY

(50¢)

BINOCULAR VIEWER

TO OPERATE TURN HANDLE ONE FULL TURN

5876

- ⊕ Focus on a middle-ground object, using the central focusing ring.

- Focus on your life vision or the point in your future where you want to be, before connecting to the next.

- ⊙ Change the lens cap so that you can see through your right eye.

- Look again, focusing now, on just your career vision.

- ⊕ With both eyes open, and staying in the same position, focus on the same object by using the diopter adjustment on the central column.

- Focus on your vision or the point in your future where you want to be, before connecting to the next.

- 👁 Remove the lens cap and enjoy the matching view through both eyes at once.

- Now, see and visualize your new career and life vision into the future.

To calibrate the diopter, you must bring the binoculars up to your eyes, open both eyes and place your right hand on the diopter. When this concept is applied to you as a Career and Life Designer, the diopter is your "pause" or reset button (it is normally set to zero); it's time to adjust. If you turn it prematurely, it makes the binoculars ineffective, as the two eyes can never focus at the same distance, at the same time. You use the binocular's central focusing knob to focus both barrels at the same time.

Then, to adjust for differences between your eyes, you use the diopter adjustment one time to fine-tune the focus for the right barrel only. Like with binoculars, you just focus on your career and get caught up in your job, or just on your personal life; you don't close one eye and squint. When the eye is squeezed closed, the pressure on your eyeball temporarily changes it shape and makes it focus differently. That, can throw your adjustment completely off. Keep both eyes open, as you should be aware of your career and life vision (together), both short-term (nearby) and long-term (far away).

From then on, the two sides will stay focused together, whether you're looking at objects near or far. This applies to your career and life vision, as they need to be assessed collectively and together, to ensure they are always balanced.

Designed by **Hassan Akmal** and Illustration by **Ahmed Zaeem**

Be yourself.

" —
  |

Forgive yourself.

  |
  — "

Conquering Your Limiting Beliefs

Let's talk about your limiting beliefs. Limiting beliefs are those which constrain us in some way. Just by believing them, we do not think, do or say the things that they inhibit. And in doing so we impoverish our lives.

How have these beliefs prevented you from pursuing goals?

What do these stories say about you and what matters most to you?

Week 1

Your Collection

You
define
success.

Happiness leads to success,
not vice-versa.

My Reflections:

TODAY I ACHIEVED...

THINGS THAT MADE ME HAPPY:

DAILY GRATITUDE LIST

INTENTION FOR TOMORROW:

NOTE TO SELF

_____

_____

_____

_____

My Reflections:

TODAY I ACHIEVED...

THINGS THAT MADE ME HAPPY:

DAILY GRATITUDE LIST

INTENTION FOR TOMORROW:

NOTE TO SELF

My Reflections:

TODAY I ACHIEVED...

DAILY GRATITUDE LIST

THINGS THAT MADE ME HAPPY:

INTENTION FOR TOMORROW:

NOTE TO SELF

My Reflections:

TODAY I ACHIEVED...

DAILY GRATITUDE LIST

THINGS THAT MADE ME HAPPY:

INTENTION FOR TOMORROW:

NOTE TO SELF

_____

_____

_____

_____

My Reflections:

TODAY I ACHIEVED...

DAILY GRATITUDE LIST

THINGS THAT MADE ME HAPPY:

INTENTION FOR TOMORROW:

NOTE TO SELF

_____

_____

_____

_____

My Reflections:

TODAY I ACHIEVED...

DAILY GRATITUDE LIST

THINGS THAT MADE ME HAPPY:

INTENTION FOR TOMORROW:

NOTE TO SELF

My Reflec+ions:

TODAY I ACHIEVED...

DAILY GRATITUDE LIST

THINGS THAT MADE ME HAPPY:

INTENTION FOR TOMORROW:

NOTE TO SELF

DATE:

_____

_____

_____

_____

_____

_____

_____

_____

_____

_____

_____

_____

NOTES

DATE:

_____

_____

_____

_____

_____

_____

_____

_____

_____

_____

_____

NOTES

_____

_____

_____

_____

_____

_____

_____

_____

_____

_____

_____

NOTES

7 Levels Deep On Your Why

By going seven levels deep, you'll discover your true "why" — the real driving force in your life.

Ask yourself again (7x), following your first answer to the following question:

What's your "why" — and why?

Week 2

Your Collection

Architectural Elements

Where you are, where you will live, and walls you might have to break down.

_____

_____

_____

_____

_____

_____

_____

_____

_____

_____

_____

_____

_____

My Reflections:

TODAY I ACHIEVED...

DAILY GRATITUDE LIST

THINGS THAT MADE ME HAPPY:

INTENTION FOR TOMORROW:

NOTE TO SELF

My Reflections:

TODAY I ACHIEVED...

DAILY GRATITUDE LIST

THINGS THAT MADE ME HAPPY:

INTENTION FOR TOMORROW:

NOTE TO SELF

My Reflections:

TODAY I ACHIEVED...

DAILY GRATITUDE LIST

THINGS THAT MADE ME HAPPY:

INTENTION FOR TOMORROW:

NOTE TO SELF

My Reflections:

TODAY I ACHIEVED...

DAILY GRATITUDE LIST

THINGS THAT MADE ME HAPPY:

INTENTION FOR TOMORROW:

NOTE TO SELF

My Reflections:

TODAY I ACHIEVED...

DAILY GRATITUDE LIST

THINGS THAT MADE ME HAPPY:

INTENTION FOR TOMORROW:

NOTE TO SELF

My Reflections:

TODAY I ACHIEVED...

DAILY GRATITUDE LIST

THINGS THAT MADE ME HAPPY:

INTENTION FOR TOMORROW:

NOTE TO SELF

My Reflections:

TODAY I ACHIEVED...

DAILY GRATITUDE LIST

THINGS THAT MADE ME HAPPY:

INTENTION FOR TOMORROW:

NOTE TO SELF

DATE:

_____

_____

_____

_____

_____

_____

_____

_____

_____

_____

_____

_____

NOTES

DATE:

_____

_____

_____

_____

_____

_____

_____

_____

_____

_____

_____

NOTES

DATE:

_____

_____

_____

_____

_____

_____

_____

_____

_____

_____

_____

NOTES

#ImpactLives

How will you use your talents to make the world a better place?

Week 3

Your Collection

Negative Spaces

Corners, holes to patch, low or tight areas to rebuild. You might need to build a bridge.

My Reflections:

TODAY I ACHIEVED...

DAILY GRATITUDE LIST

THINGS THAT MADE ME HAPPY:

INTENTION FOR TOMORROW:

NOTE TO SELF

_____

_____

_____

_____

My Reflections:

TODAY I ACHIEVED...

DAILY GRATITUDE LIST

THINGS THAT MADE ME HAPPY:

INTENTION FOR TOMORROW:

NOTE TO SELF

My Reflections:

TODAY I ACHIEVED...

DAILY GRATITUDE LIST

THINGS THAT MADE ME HAPPY:

INTENTION FOR TOMORROW:

NOTE TO SELF

My Reflections:

TODAY I ACHIEVED...

DAILY GRATITUDE LIST

THINGS THAT MADE ME HAPPY:

INTENTION FOR TOMORROW:

NOTE TO SELF

_____

_____

_____

_____

My Reflections:

TODAY I ACHIEVED...

DAILY GRATITUDE LIST

THINGS THAT MADE ME HAPPY:

INTENTION FOR TOMORROW:

NOTE TO SELF

_____

_____

_____

_____

My Reflections:

TODAY I ACHIEVED...

DAILY GRATITUDE LIST

THINGS THAT MADE ME HAPPY:

INTENTION FOR TOMORROW:

NOTE TO SELF

My Reflecíions:

TODAY I ACHIEVED...

THINGS THAT MADE ME HAPPY:

DAILY GRATITUDE LIST

INTENTION FOR TOMORROW:

NOTE TO SELF

DATE:

_____

_____

_____

_____

_____

_____

_____

_____

_____

_____

_____

NOTES

DATE:

_____

_____

_____

_____

_____

_____

_____

_____

_____

_____

_____

_____

NOTES

_____

_____

_____

_____

_____

_____

_____

_____

_____

_____

_____

NOTES

"Listen to the call of discovery.
Use it to create your Purpose.
This will lead to a wondrous life."

—*Hassan Akmal*

This Moment Is Life

"Drink your tea slowly and reverently, as if it is the axis on which the earth revolves — slowly, evenly, without rushing toward the future. Live the actual moment. Only this moment is life."

—*Thich Nhat Hanh, Vietnamese monk*

Every single moment in life — matters.

Experiences are what make life what it is, and you are a product of them. Positive or negative.

The phrase, 'ichi-go ichi-e' (一期一会), traces back to 16th-century tea ceremonies in Japan.

Tea ceremony in Pakistan: Image generated with Midjourney

Frame the
monent.

As a chai master, you cherish the 'cha' as my mom says, or tea. You perfect it, even in how you serve it to others. You prepare it with love and give it from the heart.

Something as simple as a tea ceremony can change your life as it changes you within the moments that define it. Giving a part of you is integral to the interior design of your career and life.

Every meeting is just like the first — and is the last. You must be present with the moment, as each moment is sacred. I have tried to apply this concept to my prayers in the early mornings before sunrise or late in the night when the silence is keener — trying to improve my meditation and focus. This way, I block out the waves of distraction — the illusions that surround us and focus on the moment in front of me. I call them standing moments, as they are fleeting and will never come again.

Tea ceremony in Pakistan: Image generated with Midjourney

The perspective and meaning of 'ichi-go ichi-e', give you appreciation and deep gratitude. You never take the time nor people or opportunities for granted. No matter the circumstances.

The value comes only once in a lifetime. So you have to hold on to it like a treasure, as it won't come again exactly the same.

To me, chai is art. Just like the interior design of our careers and life. One cup, like a morning routine, can change the course of the day — if you allow it to.

The saying, 'ichi-go ichi-e', was coined by Ii Naosuke, a Japanese tea master who lived from 1815-1860. Coming from another tea master (like myself), it resonated on a whole different level. But, in his case, the legend goes that he had many death threats so he prepared his tea as if it would be his last.

Every time Naosuke made tea, it was said and believed to be unique and more beautiful than the time before. He embraced and revered the impermanence of life.

With gratitude.

This is the secret to being the interior designer of your life.

It's a love like no other for the serendipity of life.

Applying this to your Pupose as well helps you recognize the beauty of serendipity and you will think twice when you receive an invitation next time.

Just think back to when you have felt an "intense presence" — for me and it's when I was in the "zone" or flow state when I am the happiest. Deep prayer and mediation, on the tennis court, writing, traveling and experiences that teach you about life, being

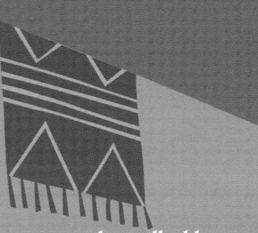

"Diversify your moments, they will add up.
The whole (you) will always be greater
than the sum of your parts —
those broken and those celebrated."

— *Hassan Akmal*

in the right company at the right time — think about yourself, when do you feel fully present?

Everything can wait except what is happening right now.

Every journey begins with a cup of tea.

It's mindset mastery — as you have to be fully self-aware.

Love yourself to free yourself. As only then, you will find yourself.

When you drink, sip the tea — feel the burning in your stomach, the pleasure of the sensation, until the last drops which are the richest drops, know as the golden drops.

It also works with green tea with lots of fresh mint inside — Moroccan style. You will feel the tingling if it's made right.

Tea ceremonies are a staple in my family. Everything matters from the cups or glasses, the pot, the stirrer or spoons, the table, the seats or cushions around the table — you name it. We don't take anything for granted.

Just like the Chinese tea master and author Lu Yu says in his classic Chinese book on tea, Ch'a Ching:

"Always sip tea as if you were sipping life itself."

In a solar eclipse, the light from the sun is obscured by the moon. However, with career and life vision, it's completely the opposite, an eclipse of the heart opens the light pathways, and your internal prisms right size the image using collimation. From there, your diopter and lenses provide the focus to bring you clarity of vision. The ability to see your future clearly depends on your career and life vision.

Sunset: La Jolla Shores, San Diego

All great change starts with influence. But, you must first influence yourself. Look within.

I believe that if you do this — your heart, mind, and soul align as *one* in an eclipse of powerful purpose.

$ Ch'a—Ching!

"Murmuration of starlings slowly taking the form of a falcon. Their connection to one another is surreal and pure, yet — each one independently matters, spiritually rising from the same tree.

Just like the moments that manifest together in your life, you become what you craft."

—Hassan Akmal

Falcon among murmuration of starlings

Images generated with Midjourney

"Believe you can and you're halfway there."

—Theodore Roosevelt

> "Inside of a ring or out, ain't nothing wrong with going down. It's staying down that's wrong."
>
> —*Muhammad Ali*

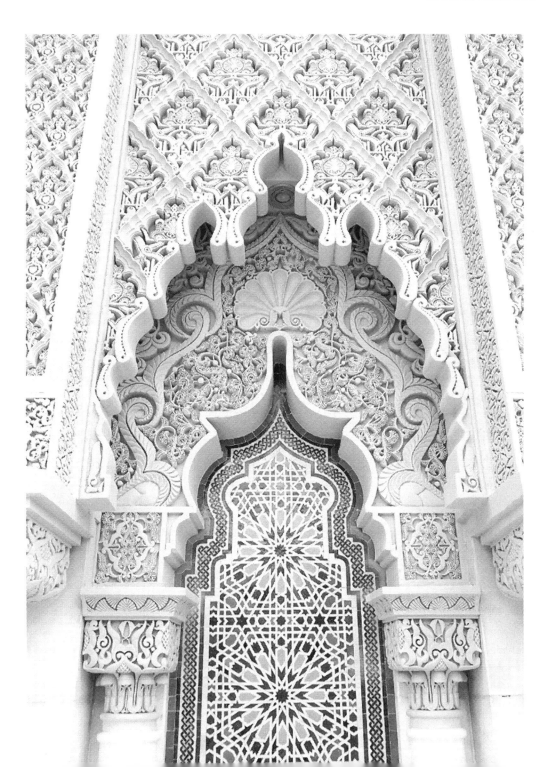

Week 4

Your Collection

Openings and Walls

I always wanted a secret door, what about you? Design your entrance and the first thing you want to see.

My Reflecíions:

TODAY I ACHIEVED...

DAILY GRATITUDE LIST

THINGS THAT MADE ME HAPPY:

INTENTION FOR TOMORROW:

NOTE TO SELF

My Reflections:

TODAY I ACHIEVED...

DAILY GRATITUDE LIST

THINGS THAT MADE ME HAPPY:

INTENTION FOR TOMORROW:

NOTE TO SELF

_____

_____

_____

_____

My Reflections:

TODAY I ACHIEVED...

DAILY GRATITUDE LIST

THINGS THAT MADE ME HAPPY:

INTENTION FOR TOMORROW:

NOTE TO SELF

My Reflections:

TODAY I ACHIEVED...

DAILY GRATITUDE LIST

THINGS THAT MADE ME HAPPY:

INTENTION FOR TOMORROW:

NOTE TO SELF

My Reflections:

TODAY I ACHIEVED...

DAILY GRATITUDE LIST

THINGS THAT MADE ME HAPPY:

INTENTION FOR TOMORROW:

NOTE TO SELF

My Reflections:

TODAY I ACHIEVED...

DAILY GRATITUDE LIST

THINGS THAT MADE ME HAPPY:

INTENTION FOR TOMORROW:

NOTE TO SELF

_____
_____
_____
_____

My Reflections:

TODAY I ACHIEVED...

DAILY GRATITUDE LIST

THINGS THAT MADE ME HAPPY:

INTENTION FOR TOMORROW:

NOTE TO SELF

DATE:

_____

_____

_____

_____

_____

_____

_____

_____

_____

_____

_____

NOTES

DATE:

_____

_____

_____

_____

_____

_____

_____

_____

_____

_____

_____

NOTES

_____

_____

_____

_____

_____

_____

_____

_____

_____

_____

_____

_____

NOTES

"Be a Prompt — Poet (AI) of Your Career and Life Design."

—*Hassan Akmal*

Week 5

Your Collection

Location: History and Future

Imagine yourself in the city that you're in or the one you want to be in. Is it private? Every community has a story.

My Reflecions:

TODAY I ACHIEVED...

DAILY GRATITUDE LIST

THINGS THAT MADE ME HAPPY:

INTENTION FOR TOMORROW:

NOTE TO SELF

My Reflecions:

TODAY I ACHIEVED...

DAILY GRATITUDE LIST

THINGS THAT MADE ME HAPPY:

INTENTION FOR TOMORROW:

NOTE TO SELF

_____

_____

_____

_____

My Reflecíions:

TODAY I ACHIEVED...

DAILY GRATITUDE LIST

THINGS THAT MADE ME HAPPY:

INTENTION FOR TOMORROW:

NOTE TO SELF

_____

_____

_____

_____

My Reflections:

TODAY I ACHIEVED...

DAILY GRATITUDE LIST

THINGS THAT MADE ME HAPPY:

INTENTION FOR TOMORROW:

NOTE TO SELF

My Reflections:

TODAY I ACHIEVED...

DAILY GRATITUDE LIST

THINGS THAT MADE ME HAPPY:

INTENTION FOR TOMORROW:

NOTE TO SELF

_____

_____

_____

_____

My Reflections:

TODAY I ACHIEVED...

DAILY GRATITUDE LIST

THINGS THAT MADE ME HAPPY:

INTENTION FOR TOMORROW:

NOTE TO SELF

_____

_____

_____

_____

My Reflections:

TODAY I ACHIEVED...

DAILY GRATITUDE LIST

THINGS THAT MADE ME HAPPY:

INTENTION FOR TOMORROW:

NOTE TO SELF

DATE:

_____

_____

_____

_____

_____

_____

_____

_____

_____

_____

_____

_____

NOTES

DATE:

_____

_____

_____

_____

_____

_____

_____

_____

_____

_____

_____

NOTES

DATE:

_____

_____

_____

_____

_____

_____

_____

_____

_____

_____

_____

_____

NOTES

IMAGINE

The mirage is real and
it's a life worth living.

Week 6

Your Collection

Sound Design

Do you wake up to the sounds of birds or a water fountain? Is it sound proof or quiet? What do you hear?

_____

_____

_____

_____

_____

_____

_____

_____

_____

_____

_____

_____

_____

_____

_____

_____

_____

_____

_____

_____

_____

_____

_____

_____

_____

_____

My Reflecions:

TODAY I ACHIEVED...

DAILY GRATITUDE LIST

THINGS THAT MADE ME HAPPY:

INTENTION FOR TOMORROW:

NOTE TO SELF

_____

_____

_____

_____

My Reflections:

TODAY I ACHIEVED...

DAILY GRATITUDE LIST

THINGS THAT MADE ME HAPPY:

INTENTION FOR TOMORROW:

NOTE TO SELF

My Reflections:

TODAY I ACHIEVED...

DAILY GRATITUDE LIST

THINGS THAT MADE ME HAPPY:

INTENTION FOR TOMORROW:

NOTE TO SELF

My Reflections:

TODAY I ACHIEVED...

DAILY GRATITUDE LIST

THINGS THAT MADE ME HAPPY:

INTENTION FOR TOMORROW:

NOTE TO SELF

My Reflections:

TODAY I ACHIEVED...

DAILY GRATITUDE LIST

THINGS THAT MADE ME HAPPY:

INTENTION FOR TOMORROW:

NOTE TO SELF

My Reflections:

TODAY I ACHIEVED...

DAILY GRATITUDE LIST

THINGS THAT MADE ME HAPPY:

INTENTION FOR TOMORROW:

NOTE TO SELF

_____

_____

_____

_____

My Reflections:

TODAY I ACHIEVED...

DAILY GRATITUDE LIST

THINGS THAT MADE ME HAPPY:

INTENTION FOR TOMORROW:

NOTE TO SELF

DATE:

_____

_____

_____

_____

_____

_____

_____

_____

_____

_____

_____

_____

NOTES

DATE:

_____

_____

_____

_____

_____

_____

_____

_____

_____

_____

_____

NOTES

_____

_____

_____

_____

_____

_____

_____

_____

_____

_____

_____

_____

NOTES

The Serendipity of Career and Life Design

I was born — en — "las montanas" — in Bozeman, Montana. Perchance, *one* with its sublime nature, from my first step as a child.

Surrounded by dynamic giants, snow-covered mountain ranges, and impressive hills that challenge the limits of any panoramic lens, I felt a profound calling and peace from a very young age. Birds used to land on my back and shoulders. There was something more to be discovered there.

Bozeman, Montana: Image created with Midjourney

I knew there was a powerful purpose whose clarity could only be grasped tangibly from the peaks of Montana's powerful and captivating mountains — that is if only one could make it to the top! But, regardless, I knew that one day my soul would unite with their broad shoulders of time, and wisdom — in all of their greatness.

That was my moment of truth, an inflection standing moment and pause — that was timeless, and that has stayed with me to this day.

In those sacred moments of reflection, and with immense gratitude, my heart traveled the entire world and came back to me and said:

"There is nobody more fortunate than you, Hassan."

I need not travel any other path, but my own.

My career and life vision was discovered there — deep within Montana's mesmerizing mysteries of beauty, its jaw-dropping impressions, and spiritually within myself.

This is where my journey to the TEDx stage really began, and this is where I will take you — as it is very much a part of my interior design and collection.

Let's look back together, and allow me to begin with a question many people ask me:

How Do You Land a TED Talk?

In short, you apply and/or get nominated. Either way, at least in my case, you must go through multiple rounds — including a lengthy application, audition reel, phone screening, panel interviews with the curation team, and if you're lucky, a final interview with the lead organizer. Sure, it's daunting — but challenges only remain challenges if your perspective doesn't change. Indeed, it was intimidating and a lot of pressure, but all of that disappeared when I visualized it next to the size and gravity of Montana's mountains. Those mountains could keep the earth from shaking during even the greatest earthquakes.

Looking up at the peaks of the forces of nature will inspire you to set new and bold goals for yourself. That's exactly what I did. I Imagined it.

No matter what life throws at you, as it's full of moments that shake you, personal and professional earthquakes — some small, some big, and your self-belief and Purpose will help you see it through.

Long ago during a "YOU Matter" Design Your Career and Life Workshop at Columbia University, I wrote the following: "Deliver a TED or TEDx Talk." This was written in a small bucket list journal I carried with me for motivation. Nobody can predict the future without a doubt, but when moments and opportunities are right, you feel them. I knew that the time for this particular opportunity would present itself when I least expected it, and it did! One of my students suggested I apply. They actually gave me the push I needed. I will forever be grateful.

We all have dreams, but sometimes our limiting beliefs can get in the way. Not acting or letting fear stop you can be more destructive in the long run than actually trying and failing. So, I acted. I applied as an alumnus to Columbia University's TEDx in September 2018. It was a formal application process. I was definitely nervous. I knew that this was at an Ivy League institution with a rich and extensive network that stretched the globe. The quality of the applicants would be top-notch. But, never cut yourself short. You must believe in yourself before anyone else. Remember, the skill of climbing mountains starts with a vision and requires *consistent persistence.*

One Big Idea That Will Change Your Life

It's tough to narrow down your concept to one big idea on your application. I decided to purchase TED's Master Class which helps you learn how to give a TED-style talk. It costs only $50. I spent the entire weekend going through it and taking notes. Not only did the course help me shape many ideas into one core concept, but it also helped me build out the first few minutes of my script that I wrote in my journal. I hadn't finished yet and was selected for an audition.

Having to answer questions off the cuff — as they throw them at you, was more rigorous than expected. Why? The questions were different and nothing I was used to as a career coach. TED has a unique brand and spirit. It's different and challenges the norm.

The process — itself, will innovate you.

One takeaway I have is that regardless if you were highly regarded on campus as a prestigious leader or a prominent alum, it didn't seem to matter. I thought I had an edge because of that, but I was wrong. What mattered was whether your idea was worth sharing. That's it. It also didn't matter if you were an author or famous. The substance mattered more and I truly appreciated this about the process.

TED is all about giving a voice to those that deserve it, who have something of value to be shared. It gives voices to the silent. Stories are powerful, their meaning has a formative and lasting impact.

Fast forward from early September to mid-November, I was a finalist. Feeling confident, I was asked to deliver part of my speech in the final round in front of a blend of students, staff, faculty, and alumni — the curation committee, as well as representatives of the TEDxColumbiaUniversity's Organizing Team. There were 7-10 people in total. They asked for the first minute and a half of my speech, but I had four minutes prepared (just in case). I was also told that the theme for the event was "Action Potential" — so this was something I stitched in. In fact, I spent a great deal of time continuously refining my opening statements and "hook" — as I knew that would be a strong determining factor ultimately on how well my TEDx Talk might perform. The auditions went by so fast, like the blink of an eye, and before I could really let it all sink in — it was over. Now, I just had to wait patiently for the selection announcement.

Fast forward: I wasn't selected.

Yes, you heard right — I didn't get it. Well, I tried my best. I couldn't help but to second-guess — not only my idea but my preparation and delivery. Eventually, with the help of one of my mastermind groups, I lifted myself up and re-focused. Upon hearing some helpful constructive feedback from the curation team, in terms of the quality of my delivery and idea being very strong, I decided to just, let - it - go. Knowing how robust the selection process was, and that there were applications from all over the world — getting so close that I could taste victory really made it difficult to accept. I actually didn't think that (in the future) it would be in cards for me, and I accepted that — as is. Despite moving on, I felt like I had let myself down and my family. Eventually I "forgave" myself and moved on, setting a new goal that one day I would publish my first book before ever considering I reapply. I asked myself, what can I do to elevate my brand?

Chaos and Happenstance, or Planned Happenstance?

I have always been drawn to theories of career development that acknowledge the impact of outside influences, unexpected, or chance events on our careers. Theories such as Chaos and Happenstance, Chaos Theory of Careers, or Planned Happenstance intrigue me, as I know that "life happens" — and whether luck happens or not, I have always believed that you can improve the chances of things going your way with a positive mindset. Mind over matter, right? This is why I created a positivity diary.

With my inner spirit laser-focused on building and expanding my digital footprint, I mapped out a new plan. My strategy?

Give back without expecting anything in return and the rewards would come back to me organically and multifold.

I started immediately. I gave out free advice, left and right. I also began a YouTube Channel entitled: "Career and Life Mastery" — this was all part of my international design.

Immersed in my network, I tried to build value with every new and existing relationship. The hard work finally paid off. After "sponsoring" my friend Mark for a speaking gig, I asked if he knew anyone that might be interested in reading and reviewing my book. He said, "I actually do know someone!" He offered to introduce me.

It sounded too good to be true, but it wasn't.

The next thing I knew is that I was on the phone with an intellectual genius, who dazzled me with each word. And a few days later, a gift package arrived with my name on it. It was from Richard Saul Wurman, the Creator of TED. It was his new book: *Understanding Understanding*.

Photo of gift from Richard Saul Wurman

I first met Richard in 2018. I was awe-struck by his unique ability to see things differently, and his passion to make learning more interesting. After winning the Smithsonian Lifetime Achievement Award, he graciously accepted my offer to read and review my book, *How to be a Career Mastermind™: Discover 7 "YOU Matter" Lenses for a Life of Purpose, Impact, and Meaningful Work.*

This man was a rare find and extremely humble. His metaphors? They were jaw-dropping! With each conversation I had with him, I learned something new. He challenged me. I even remember him telling me that the graduation ceremony in higher education needed to be reinvented! He argued that it needs to be much more enjoyable (and not stressful). There is too much waiting around! Don't you all tend to agree with him? I know I do!

I admired how Richard would describe to me that his path was "chosen for him" — this fascinated me. He motivated me too, in the designing of career and life.

Richard said that he would be happy to read my book and write a review. I was flattered and humbled! Can you believe, he read the entire book? I couldn't believe it. Following, he called me to read his review — aloud and wanted me to write it down on the spot. Again, so humbling and motivating. Here is what he wrote in his review:

"Finally, an academic who focuses on learning — rather than education. I can't type. This failure of mine has led me to recording my thoughts and having them transcribed. I decided not to take notes, which led to an enormous improvement in my memory connecting what I hear to other experiences and knowledge and a visual mental web of understanding. Both of these things have become a piece of the design in my life. This book is quite a surprise to me, not only because its author is an academic, but also in its endorsement of passionately designing your life. The big design problem is the design of your life. Not the design of a car, or a house or even a curriculum — it is the design of your life. What you do in your life takes up most of your day and that design should not be left to others. This is a book about participating in your own learning. It is a remarkable, passionate guidebook — dense, but easily absorbed because you hear this rather wondrous man talking to you as you read. It feels like he is sitting next to you and delivering this wisdom for your understanding and your memory without notes; without a typewriter, without the formality of the educational system, giving you a plan that leads to the design of a personal learning system. I particularly like his metaphors about tennis — I congratulate him on his efforts!"

— *RICHARD SAUL WURMAN*

CREATOR OF TED; AUTHOR OF OVER 90 BOOKS ON WILDLY DIVERGENT TOPICS; CONTRIBUTOR TO GENIUS: 100 VISIONS OF THE FUTURE, SPONSORED BY THE EINSTEIN LEGACY PROJECT, WHICH FEATURES ESSAYS SUBMITTED BY THE 100 GREATEST INNOVATORS, ARTISTS, SCIENTISTS

Richard didn't know that I had applied to be a TEDx speaker, nor that I wasn't selected. I was ashamed to tell him. But then, I asked myself:

What are the chances that I would meet the Creator of TED? The serendipity of life.

I took this as a sign! After telling him, Richard felt that I had a strong idea and message to share. His belief that I was TED material inspired me to one day reapply. Regardless of whether it would be a TED Talk or a TEDx Talk, I knew that this time around, I would meticulously prepare for the audition and interviews with the competition being as steep as it was before. I mean, I did well before, but I needed to take it to the next level to land the talk.

I was speaking to the man himself, who's shoulders I would stand on, who's vision could only be seen on the peaks of mountains.

Inspired by Richard, I began to look at things differently. Instead of my perspective being what happened *to* me, I looked at things now happening *for* me. It was a blessing with a dressing, as my performance would only improve. Maybe I wouldn't have done as well in my talk if I would have gotten it the first time around? Perhaps this was God's way of helping me shine? Things were looking brighter, so I kept my "inner" self in check with positive reinforcements and an unshakeable mindset.

RE—Vision, RE—Focus

When it comes to impressing a curation team that has gone through hundreds of applications, it's important to not be over confident. What's very critical too is the diversity of topics — as they align with the theme of the event. I remember being told that the "self-help" category was extremely competitive with thousands of interested contenders with proposals related to finding success, happiness or purpose. However, I didn't let that discourage me. Before I could reapply, I was notified that I had been nominated. Thus, I began writing my speech when the new theme was announced: RE-Vision, RE-Focus. That same moment I finalized the title of my talk, but kept it a secret.

TEDx Performance — Lincoln Center, New York City: March 27, 2021

The event was TBA in 2020. I submitted my application in late 2019 and went through another tough 7-8 rounds of screening, auditions and interviews. Every TEDx organizing team is different — they have similar, but different processes. It may be easier at other locations. However, mine was nerve-racking and exceptionally challenging. But, this time — I felt like I passed each round with flying colors. The only difference for me was that mentally, I was much more confident than last time. However, it's tough to really know where you stand in the process as it progresses, as you don't know exactly what they are looking for. The topics of speakers can be very broad and apply to many audiences — they cut across many diverse disciplines. So, I didn't know what or who I was up against. After my final round, I left it all in the Hands of the Almighty. The next day, I wrote my best thank you email ever. And then, the call came.

"Congratulations on being selected as a TEDx Speaker!"

This was incredible news. I was speechless. The event date was originally slotted for May 2020. The venue, the prestigious Lincoln Center in New York City! But then, the pandemic happened. It was postponed indefinitely. Just my luck! All of the speakers were announced in early 2020, and we were all very anxious. We asked ourselves and each other, what if the event is cancelled? Would we lose one of the greatest opportunities of our lives? We were hopeful and prayed — no, I mean literally!

The new date was eventually announced, and the preparations were in high gear. This, in theory, gave us more time to prepare. But, in reality, none of us really began writing our speeches as we didn't know if the event would ever take place.

Five Tips for Aspiring TED Speakers

According to the Washington Post, fear of public speaking is America's biggest phobia - 25.3 percent say they fear speaking in front of a crowd. Below is a list of some of the things I focused on to help me overcome any fear, for what felt like — the most important speech of my life.

1. Be Self-Aware: Rehearse and Record Your Tone, Pace, and Hand Gestures

One TEDx Talk I highly recommend is entitled: The 110 techniques of communication and public speaking. It's by David JP Phillips. It's very helpful, and entertaining. Enjoy!

2. Go Seven Levels Deep on Your Why

Most people thing they know their "Why," but they are far from it. Ask yourself, "but why?" If you do that enough times, eventually you will get down to it and it will be a game-changer, I promise.

3. Progress Versus Perfection

Write your speech out. Jot down your thoughts wherever you are. Especially when you wake up with them, before you forget. Use an app to save great and inspiring quotes. Keep the ideas flowing.

4. Watch as Many TED Talks as Possible

I must have watched over 100 talks before I gave mine. Some of the talks I watched multiple times. Here is one of my favorites. It's called: "The Gift and Power of Emotional Courage."

Psychologist Susan David shares how the way we deal with our emotions shapes everything that matters: our actions, careers, relationships, health and happiness. In this deeply moving, humorous and potentially life-changing talk, she challenges a culture that prizes positivity over emotional truth and discusses the powerful strategies of emotional agility.

Her perspective on being positive and how it impacts moral correctness is eye-opening and life-changing. Agility is highly underestimated — a success and career readiness skill for now, more than ever, and the future.

5. Be YOU

Don't try to be anyone else. It will show. This is your moment, not someone else's. Tell your story and let your heart carry it into other hearts.

The event was announced. It was happening! It didn't get cancelled. It felt like I was getting married and my wedding day — like I was racing against time to prepare my speech and wedding vows!

Regardless of whether you attend a TED event, speak on stage, or just watch from the comfort of your own home, I encourage you to embrace the TED Spirit. "TED" stands for *Technology, Entertainment,* and *Design.* TED is a global community, welcoming people from every discipline and culture who seek a deeper understanding of the world. They believe passionately in the power of ideas to change attitudes, lives and, ultimately, the world. Become a member. I hope you have found this story insightful. The lessons will also apply to your career and life design.

One Parting Thought

"Let your subconscious mind and heart be the drivers in your life, they are already thousands of steps ahead of you! Let them lead the sacred caravan to the future."

— Hassan Akmal

There you will find me. There, I will wait for you.

As for me, what's next on my bucket list?

I vow to go back to Bozeman, Montana — to see, once again, the mountains that inspired me — moving my heart closer in my spiritual journey — *home.*

Falcon: Image created with Midjourney

"Masters of the sky" accompany me on the path of discovery.

The poetic falcons' cries will pierce your ears and hearts. Their wings roam free through the commanding prominence of glorious kings of nature, surrounding them with speed, grace, agility and high-velocity.

There you will find me. There, I will wait for you.

Make the moon
a part of your design.

Week 7

Your Collection

Molding, Materials, and Textures

Patterns, sequences, how it feels, and what inspires you?

My Reflections:

TODAY I ACHIEVED...

DAILY GRATITUDE LIST

THINGS THAT MADE ME HAPPY:

INTENTION FOR TOMORROW:

NOTE TO SELF

_____

_____

_____

_____

My Reflecions:

TODAY I ACHIEVED...

DAILY GRATITUDE LIST

THINGS THAT MADE ME HAPPY:

INTENTION FOR TOMORROW:

NOTE TO SELF

My Reflecions:

TODAY I ACHIEVED...

DAILY GRATITUDE LIST

THINGS THAT MADE ME HAPPY:

INTENTION FOR TOMORROW:

NOTE TO SELF

_____

_____

_____

_____

My Reflections:

TODAY I ACHIEVED...

DAILY GRATITUDE LIST

THINGS THAT MADE ME HAPPY:

INTENTION FOR TOMORROW:

NOTE TO SELF

_____

_____

_____

_____

My Reflections:

TODAY I ACHIEVED...

DAILY GRATITUDE LIST

THINGS THAT MADE ME HAPPY:

INTENTION FOR TOMORROW:

NOTE TO SELF

_____
_____
_____
_____

My Reflections:

TODAY I ACHIEVED...

DAILY GRATITUDE LIST

THINGS THAT MADE ME HAPPY:

INTENTION FOR TOMORROW:

NOTE TO SELF

My Reflecüons:

TODAY I ACHIEVED...

THINGS THAT MADE ME HAPPY:

DAILY GRATITUDE LIST

INTENTION FOR TOMORROW:

NOTE TO SELF

_____

_____

_____

_____

_____

_____

_____

_____

_____

_____

_____

_____

NOTES

DATE:

_____

_____

_____

_____

_____

_____

_____

_____

_____

_____

_____

_____

NOTES

DATE:

_____

_____

_____

_____

_____

_____

_____

_____

_____

_____

_____

_____

_____

NOTES

Dream Bigger.

Cappadocia

Week 8

Your Collection

The Brilliance is in the Details

Recreate the details you love. Everything is connected to you. In fact, you are having a dialogue with one another.

My Reflections:

TODAY I ACHIEVED...

DAILY GRATITUDE LIST

THINGS THAT MADE ME HAPPY:

INTENTION FOR TOMORROW:

NOTE TO SELF

My Reflections:

TODAY I ACHIEVED...

DAILY GRATITUDE LIST

THINGS THAT MADE ME HAPPY:

INTENTION FOR TOMORROW:

NOTE TO SELF

My Reflections:

TODAY I ACHIEVED...

DAILY GRATITUDE LIST

THINGS THAT MADE ME HAPPY:

INTENTION FOR TOMORROW:

NOTE TO SELF

_____

_____

_____

_____

My Reflections:

TODAY I ACHIEVED...

DAILY GRATITUDE LIST

THINGS THAT MADE ME HAPPY:

INTENTION FOR TOMORROW:

NOTE TO SELF

My Reflections:

TODAY I ACHIEVED...

DAILY GRATITUDE LIST

THINGS THAT MADE ME HAPPY:

INTENTION FOR TOMORROW:

NOTE TO SELF

_____
_____
_____
_____

My Reflections:

TODAY I ACHIEVED...

DAILY GRATITUDE LIST

THINGS THAT MADE ME HAPPY:

INTENTION FOR TOMORROW:

NOTE TO SELF

My Reflections:

TODAY I ACHIEVED... ✦

DAILY GRATITUDE LIST

THINGS THAT MADE ME HAPPY:

INTENTION FOR TOMORROW:

NOTE TO SELF

_____
_____
_____
_____

_____

_____

_____

_____

_____

_____

_____

_____

_____

_____

_____

_____

NOTES

DATE:

_____

_____

_____

_____

_____

_____

_____

_____

_____

_____

_____

NOTES

DATE:

_____

_____

_____

_____

_____

_____

_____

_____

_____

_____

_____

_____

_____

NOTES

Redefining the Word "Career"

What's your definition of a career?

Using your new definition of a career and/or of multiple careers, create a Career Bucket List.

Prioritize them.

Week 9

Your Collection

The Lighting

Lighting provides wayfinding. We are all way finders. Create signage and design elements to help you navigate.

_____

_____

_____

_____

_____

_____

_____

_____

_____

_____

_____

_____

_____

My Reflecíions:

TODAY I ACHIEVED...

DAILY GRATITUDE LIST

THINGS THAT MADE ME HAPPY:

INTENTION FOR TOMORROW:

NOTE TO SELF

_____

_____

_____

_____

My Reflections:

TODAY I ACHIEVED...

DAILY GRATITUDE LIST

THINGS THAT MADE ME HAPPY:

INTENTION FOR TOMORROW:

NOTE TO SELF

My Reflections:

TODAY I ACHIEVED...

DAILY GRATITUDE LIST

THINGS THAT MADE ME HAPPY:

INTENTION FOR TOMORROW:

NOTE TO SELF

My Reflections:

TODAY I ACHIEVED...

DAILY GRATITUDE LIST

THINGS THAT MADE ME HAPPY:

INTENTION FOR TOMORROW:

NOTE TO SELF

My Reflections:

TODAY I ACHIEVED...

DAILY GRATITUDE LIST

THINGS THAT MADE ME HAPPY:

INTENTION FOR TOMORROW:

NOTE TO SELF

My Reflections:

TODAY I ACHIEVED...

DAILY GRATITUDE LIST

THINGS THAT MADE ME HAPPY:

INTENTION FOR TOMORROW:

NOTE TO SELF

My Reflections:

TODAY I ACHIEVED...

DAILY GRATITUDE LIST

THINGS THAT MADE ME HAPPY:

INTENTION FOR TOMORROW:

NOTE TO SELF

DATE:

_____

_____

_____

_____

_____

_____

_____

_____

_____

_____

_____

_____

NOTES

DATE:

_____

_____

_____

_____

_____

_____

_____

_____

_____

_____

_____

_____

_____

NOTES

DATE:

_____

_____

_____

_____

_____

_____

_____

_____

_____

_____

_____

_____

NOTES

You Can't Be What You Can't See

Fill your heart with true faith — and you will be able to see the future.

With the true and deep confidence that you can achieve your dreams, recreate your life bucket list.

Week 10

Your Collection

Colors

Play with the colors. Which ones will you celebrate? Find your inner voice and tell your story with color.

My Reflections:

TODAY I ACHIEVED...

DAILY GRATITUDE LIST

THINGS THAT MADE ME HAPPY:

INTENTION FOR TOMORROW:

NOTE TO SELF

My Reflections:

TODAY I ACHIEVED...

DAILY GRATITUDE LIST

THINGS THAT MADE ME HAPPY:

INTENTION FOR TOMORROW:

NOTE TO SELF

My Reflections:

TODAY I ACHIEVED...

DAILY GRATITUDE LIST

THINGS THAT MADE ME HAPPY:

INTENTION FOR TOMORROW:

NOTE TO SELF

My Reflecions:

TODAY I ACHIEVED...

DAILY GRATITUDE LIST

THINGS THAT MADE ME HAPPY:

INTENTION FOR TOMORROW:

NOTE TO SELF

My Reflecions:

TODAY I ACHIEVED...

DAILY GRATITUDE LIST

THINGS THAT MADE ME HAPPY:

INTENTION FOR TOMORROW:

NOTE TO SELF

_____

_____

_____

_____

My Reflections:

TODAY I ACHIEVED...

DAILY GRATITUDE LIST

THINGS THAT MADE ME HAPPY:

INTENTION FOR TOMORROW:

NOTE TO SELF

My Reflections:

TODAY I ACHIEVED...

DAILY GRATITUDE LIST

THINGS THAT MADE ME HAPPY:

INTENTION FOR TOMORROW:

NOTE TO SELF

DATE:

_____

_____

_____

_____

_____

_____

_____

_____

_____

_____

_____

_____

NOTES

DATE:

_____

_____

_____

_____

_____

_____

_____

_____

_____

_____

_____

_____

NOTES

_____

_____

_____

_____

_____

_____

_____

_____

_____

_____

_____

_____

NOTES

Increase the Conviction That YOU Matter

Purpose exists at the crossroads of what you are passionate about and where your talents lie.

Liberate your interior design collection by transforming your vision into Purpose — one that the world needs and will cherish.

Design Your Thinking

Now it's time to revisit the 7 "YOU Matter" Purpose Lenses. You have had time to think about them as they apply to your career and life blueprint, designs, and collections. Let's quickly review some key points.

What is design thinking? I define it as "designing your thinking" — it's everywhere and has been around for 20-plus years. It's a philosophy and a set of tools to help you solve problems creatively. And within that creative realm, it really looks at the human-centered side of creative problem-solving and design.

Design thinking helps you innovate and also helps you reframe, with a bias to action. It's a flexible process and the steps are meant to be broad.

Step 1 is self-empathizing, gathering information, and understanding the subject, so if applied to careers and life — it's you.

Step 2 builds off of step 1 and the insight by asking: What are we taking from that? What is the problem that we are trying to solve?

Step 3 is to ideate, and now you are building on the first two steps and coming up with ideas and matching solutions. You are brainstorming and imagining.

Step 4 is the prototype phase, and here you are breaking it all down — the ideas, then translating them into simple testable solutions. You are building your hypothesis.

Step 5 is testing. Taking the prototypes and seeing if they work, getting feedback, and then it will lead you to go back into the cycle with new data and observations — it's an iterative process to innovate and improve your design.

Life is not merely about change, but also sustainability. We want our designs to last and make an impact. Remember the Ikigai. Imagine putting change and sustainability in the center. These concepts go hand-in-hand. Mastering your visualization and crafting a human story to inspire others to take action is the last step of the design thinking approach to your career and life.

Remember, building a life you love is not going to be easy. You will need to rely on the methodologies I shared and on your ability to be intuitive. You will need to recognize patterns and form ideas that are meaningful. The ideas you construct must also be functional.

Like the "YOU Matter" Lenses, the elements of each of the five steps of design thinking depend on one another. You will make mistakes, and you will fail. Accept it; it's part of the process. Thomas Edison said, *"I failed my way to success."*

Now it's your turn. It will take time to master the design-thinking process for your career and life. For now, frame a question. Go ahead. Write it down. Make sure it is a driving question.

It's time to transform engagement into action. Every day, for the next seven days, complete one of the next 7 worksheets. If you want to take extra time to think about your answers, take the time you need.

TURN TO CLEAR VISION

CHECKLIST ITEM 1

POSITIVE MINDSET
ALMOST EVERYTHING IS PERSPECTIVE

▶ **Define where you are now:** (check one)

○ Positive   ○ Unsure   ○ Negative

▶ **Follow Up Date:**

☐ / ☐ / ☐

▶ *Why do you feel this way?*

▶ **Ikigai is seen as the convergence of 4 primary elements:**

• What you love (your passion)?

• What the world needs (your mission)?

• What you are good at (your vocation)?

• What you can get paid for (your profession)?

Discovering your own Ikigai is said to bring fulfillment, happiness and make you live longer.

▶ **Action Item:**

I will ☐

by the Date ☐ / ☐ / ☐

▶ **Completed:** (circle one)

○ Yes   ○ No

▶ *What is the "IMPACT" action you will take within one week to make a positive change?*

▶ **Want to find your Ikigai?**
Ask yourself the following 4 questions:

1. What do I love?

2. What am I good at?

3. What can I be paid for now — or something that I could transform into my future hustle?

4. What does the world need?

Circle where you are now in your life: ▶

Venn diagram showing: What you LOVE, What the world NEEDS, What you are GOOD AT, What you can be PAID FOR. Intersections labeled PASSION, MISSION, PROFESSION, VOCATION, with Ikigai at the center.

Next Steps and Notes:

CHECKLIST ITEM 2

THE UNLOCK:
CAREER AND LIFE VISION

▶ **Define where you are now:** (check all that apply)

○ My career vision is unlocked

○ My life vision is unlocked

▶ **Follow Up Date:**

☐ / ☐ / ☐

▶ *Why do you feel this way?*

▶ **Action Item:**

I will ☐

by the Date ☐ / ☐ / ☐

▶ **Completed:** (circle one)

○ Yes   ○ No

▶ *What is the "IMPACT" action you will take within one week to make a positive change?*

Career

Life

Next Steps and Notes:

CHECKLIST ITEM 3

DISCOVERY CALLS
THE PURPOSE IN YOU

▶ **Define where you are now:** (check one)

- ☐ I know my purpose
- ☐ I don't know or understand my purpose

▶ **Follow Up Date:**

☐ / ☐ / ☐

▶ *Why do you feel this way?*

▶ **Action Item:**

I will _____

by the Date ☐ / ☐ / ☐

▶ **Completed:** (circle one)

○ Yes   ○ No

▶ *What is the "IMPACT" action you will take within one week to make a positive change?*

IDEATE

Next Steps and Notes:

CHECKLIST ITEM 4

CAREER MANIFESTÓ

BE AN ARCHITECT, BUILD THE LIFE YOU LOVE

Career Bucket List

▶ **Define where you are now:** (check one)

☐ I am designing my life

☐ Someone else is designing my life

▶ **Follow Up Date:**

☐ / ☐ / ☐

▶ *Why do you feel this way?*

[ ]

▶ **Action Item:**

I will [ ]

by the Date ☐ / ☐ / ☐

▶ **Completed:** (circle one)

○ Yes   ○ No

▶ *What is the "IMPACT" action you will take within one week to make a positive change?*

[ ]

Career Ladders

HOW DO I WANT TO BE REMEMBERED?

Reflecting on my retirement speech

Life Crane

TEENAGE YEARS AND COLLEGE

Preparing for the life I want to live

My Evolving World View

I DON'T WANT TO GROW UP YEARS

No worries in the world!

I AM:
(click all that apply)

☐ Single

☐ Taken

☐ Building my empire

Next Steps and Notes:

[ ]

"YOU Matter"

CHECKLIST ITEM 5

"YOU MATTER"
WHY YOU SHOULD INVEST IN YOURSELF

▶ **Define where you are now:** (check one)

☐ I am worth it

☐ I am not worth it

▶ **Follow Up Date:**

☐ / ☐ / ☐

▶ *Why do you feel this way?*

[ ]

▶ **Action Item:**

I will [ ]

by the Date ☐ / ☐ / ☐

▶ **Completed:** (circle one)

○ Yes   ○ No

▶ *What is the "IMPACT" action you will take within one week to make a positive change?*

[ ]

"The formulation of a problem is often more essential than its solution."
–Albert Einstein

SELF - EMPATHIZE
Brainstorm potential solutions; select and develop your solution

DEFINE
Clearly articulate the problem you want to solve

IDEATE
Develop a deep understanding of the challenge

PROTOTYPE
Design a prototype (a series of prototypes) to test all part of your solution

TEST
Engage in a continuous short-cycle innovation process to continually improve your career design

Next Steps and Notes:

[ ]

My Personal Business Plan
1.
2.
3.
BIG BOSS

CHECKLIST ITEM 6

YOUR OWN PERSONAL BUSINESS PLAN

▶ **Define where you are now:** (check one)

- [ ] I have one ready-to-go
- [ ] Don't have one or I am struggling

▶ **Follow Up Date:**

[ ] / [ ] / [ ]

▶ **Why do you feel this way?**

▶ **Action Item:**

I will [ ]

by the Date [ ] / [ ] / [ ]

▶ **Completed:** (circle one)

○ Yes   ○ No

▶ **What is the "IMPACT" action you will take within one week to make a positive change?**

5 Life Design Strategies:

- [ ] Test drive your future
- [ ] Trust your gut
- [ ] Play to your strengths
- [ ] Craft your job
- [ ] Shop for the right boss

"Balance your future: your career and life visions should be evenly distributed"

Design Your Career Crown, by "walking your calling"

Next Steps and Notes:

CHECKLIST ITEM 7

A NOBLE CAREER AND MORAL COMPASS

▶ **Define where you are now:** (check one)

☐ On the right and straight path

☐ I don't know where I'm going

▶ **Follow Up Date:**

☐ / ☐ / ☐

▶ *Why do you feel this way?*

▶ **Action Item:**

I will ☐

by the Date ☐ / ☐ / ☐

▶ **Completed:** (circle one)

○ Yes ○ No

▶ *What is the "IMPACT" action you will take within one week to make a positive change?*

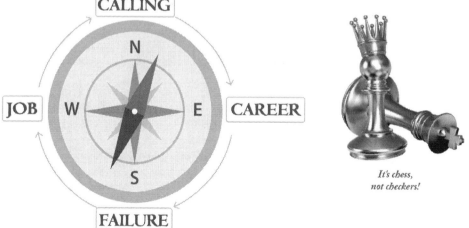

CALLING

N

JOB W · E CAREER

S

FAILURE

It's chess, not checkers!

Next Steps and Notes:

Find Your Focus.

"Forgive him who wrongs you; join him who cuts you off; do good to him who does evil to you; and speak the truth even if it be against yourself."

— Inscribed on the Prophet Muhammad's Sword
(May Peace and Blessings be Upon Him)

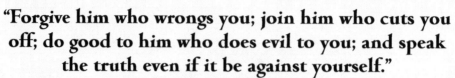

Design Your Perfect Day

Where would you be? What would you do? Who would be with you?

Design

YOUR MORNING RITUAL

Design

YOUR EVENING RITUAL

Conclusion:

— ◆◆ —

Master Your Vision

We are all entrepreneurs. It's the entre-pre-NEW-reality.

I never thought of myself as an entrepreneur. You probably don't think of yourself that way either. But eventually, I had to make a mindset shift that required me to adopt an entrepreneurial perspective. This mindset put me in the driver's seat. It means that even if I just have one career — at any given time, that employer is just my biggest client. I'm still open to more possibilities and striving toward my full potential.

Just like the spirit of TED inspired me, you will find your inspiration in many things and the experiences you create for yourself. This is your life — your own business. And so, you have to think about this design challenge like an entrepreneur.

As such, so are interior designers. They are also entrepreneurs who focus on solving design problems. So, I want you to always consider yourself as the interior designer of your career and life.

Living is Giving

Start with gratitude.

Gratitude leads to appreciation.

Appreciation leads to giving.

Giving leads to meaning.

Meaning leads to purpose.

Aligning Your Freedom

What problems are you trying to solve? These questions start you on an entrepreneurial journey of building a "startup" centered around yourself and your Purpose.

Now that you have started your career and life design collection — your personal and professional business plan — it's time to iterate and refine it until it clicks and works. It will, just give it time and keep at it. You can hire career consultants and mentors to help you, but this is your business to run and you have to own it.

Your target audience is your inner self. You are designing this sacred space for yourself so that you can hear your real voice. You start with your base self. In this new space — there, your intuition will guide you to your true and best self.

How do you design your career and life? You begin with mindfulness and reflection.

Mindfulness is central to mastering mindset and is the human ability to be fully present — aware of where you are and what you are doing, and not merely reactive to what's going on around you. It starts with your intentions. You have to purify them each morning as they will help you achieve clarity in your vision.

Once you have clarity, you can focus. Not just focus — but deep, refocusing. Writing in this journal will help you gather and organize your thoughts. It will also help you sharpen your vision. As I stated in my book, *How to be a Career Mastermind™: Discover 7 "YOU Matter" Lenses for a Life of Purpose, Impact, and Meaningful Work,* the sky is not your limit, your "North Star" is. But — you must be able to see it!

Career and life mastery is self-mastery. You are learning the ability to understand yourself — your (own) definition of a happy and meaningful life. Embedded in that vision is the idea that understanding yourself is the primary challenge in front of you. This understanding will deepen over time and help you master your visualization.

How you design your career and life begins with how you design each day. Each day is a part of your journey. Just as you clear the path when you walk, you must clear your vision every day.

Write your thoughts and aspirations in this journal. Be grateful and celebrate your wins, whether big or small.

Reach Your C-Sharp

In music, sharp, dièse (from French), or diesis (from Greek) means higher in pitch. More specifically, in musical notation, sharp means "higher in pitch by one semitone (half step)." Sharp is the opposite of flat, which is a lowering of pitch.

You have to reach for your C-Sharp. It's not at arm's length. It's like climbing a mountain. It's at its peak. Remember, the sky is not the limit, your "North Star" is.

This all takes practice and deep focus. Some people can hit it easier than others, but this lesson is not about vocals, it's about vision.

Masters of Visualization

One of my favorite opera singers, Andrea Bocelli, makes a living hitting (and breaking) this tremendous note. This legend, someone who was losing sight as a child, is a perfect example of someone who sees with his heart as he closes his eyes. He argues that musical curiosity has never abandoned him. When I listen to his voice, especially in songs like "Por ti volare" — it's almost like he's exploring his curiosity in his words. As if he's living and telling a story — at the same time. He stacks all of his feelings and emotions, relating them one by one to his life experiences. He says:

"Singing provides a true sense of lightheartedness. If I sing when I am alone, I feel wonderful. It's freedom."

You too are living and telling your story with each day. As you enter your future, enter with an infinite mindset. Enter on the path to freedom.

Your "See-Sharp" is what we are really examining here. To *see-sharper* means to see with more clarity and at greater distances as you refocus your collective life lenses and clear your path forward.

The symbol of C-Sharp looks like a hashtag, only with a slight tilt. It's within the spaces of the symbol where I would like you to focus your attention.

THE SKY IS NOT THE LIMIT

Find Your C-Sharp

- LIFE VISION
- PURPOSE
- CAREER VISION
- MORAL COMPASS
- MINDSET
- STORY TELLER+ STORY MAKER & CHANGER
- LIFE BUCKET LIST
- LEGACY
- CAREER BUCKET LIST

Above the Trend

"See-Sharp" (C-Sharp)

Designed by **Hassan Akmal**
Illustration by **Ahmed Zaeem**

Carving Out Your Space

As you progress through your interior design collections and the diverse facets of your visualization, keep in mind that the inflection moments are the most critical ones. This is called, "autobiographical planning" — when you reflect back into your life and examine the space you are in now. Here are five tips:

1. Take note of the big moments and events that changed your careers and life.

2. Think organically and naturally feel where you are internally in the design process.

3. Go beyond the conscious mind into your subconscious.

4. Create your own narrative of your career and life vision.

5. Be creative and imaginative — focus on solving challenges in your career and life design.

We shift our attention every minute, sometimes every few seconds. We check email more times than we remember ourselves. We change tasks more than we breathe in and out deeply. Take that pause now and as many times as you need going forward. Unlock your inner voice and enable it to roam freely.

Many people tell me that I should be an interior designer. As friends visit, come over for dinner, and see my place — including my catio, they usually walk away feeling inspired to design their own home or apartment. What I realized early on about myself — seeing their expressions, is that my love for interior design isn't about designing careers for other people, but instead, empowering them to be the artist of their own lives. That's my real love and craft.

I hope that through my book and this guide, you will accept the lifelong charge and honor to be the chief architect of all of your careers — the artist of your life, and the designer of rest of your life. The journey will set you free.

IMAGINE
YOUR CAREER AND LIFE VISION

VISUALIZATION

How might your life unfold if you
change nothing? What if you take risks?

Visualize different pathways in your life.

IDEATION

Does the path you're on now lead you
to where you want to go? Yes or no?

If not, it's time to change something.

PATH #1

Your story,
told by someone else.

PATH #2

The story you tell yourself,
about yourself.

PATH #3

Your true story,
the one that matters.

PATH 1 TO MEANINGFUL WORK
Describe it here.

PATH 2 TO MEANINGFUL WORK
Describe it here.

PATH 3 TO MEANINGFUL WORK
Describe it here.

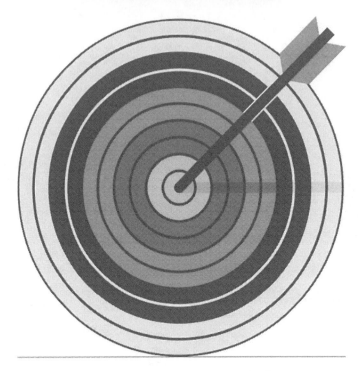

"To master your career and life, you must master your vision. A true visionary sees his target with his heart."

—HASSAN AKMAL

www.CareerandLifeMastery.com
#CareerMastermind

I aspire to be..

Path I

Path 2

Path 3

Alt.

"

LOVE YOURSELF TO FREE YOURSELF. ONLY THEN, YOU WILL FIND YOURSELF."

—HASSAN AKMAL

HASSAN AKMAL.COM

Your Retirement Speech

Imagine you are writing your retirement speech. How do you want to be remembered?

Write down thoughts on what you would like to have said about you at a dinner honoring you 20, 30, or 40 years from now.

Questions to consider asking yourself:

What and/or whom did I impact or change? What were my major accomplishments?

What did I show dedication or commitment to? What was I passionate or enthusiastic about?

What character traits and values did I consistently demonstrate over my lifetime?

Turn To Clear Your Vision

Congratulations on completing the Interior Design of Your Career and Life™. Let us not forget that to master your life, you must master your career. This is not just about career and alignment, but aligning vision and purpose. You will target and transform your life in more ways than one to impact the lives of others. This is a movement. It's also a community. The *#ImpactLives* members and the Career & Life Design community find their keys to success, open the doors to meaning, and redefine their purpose. Their lives are not happy — but joyous, because they have crafted them and because they have designed them. Thus they have championed their careers and built a new career and life vision — a holistic perspective. Seeing with their heart, they see selflessly, and this enables them to see clearly. They can see humanity. *Can you?*

Turn to change your perspectives. Turn to clear your vision. See your life in a new panoramic view. See far away and into the future. Find peace, give back, and love where it is waiting for you.

"Books change us. Books save us. I know this because it happened to me. Books saved me. So I do believe, through stories we can learn to change, we can learn to empathize and be more connected with the universe and with humanity."

— Elif Safak

Coin operated binoculars with view of New York and Empire State Building

FREE LIVE ONLINE TRAINING

Discover 7 "YOU Matter" Lenses for a Life of Purpose, Impact, and Meaningful Work

Visit www.CareerandLife.Vision/webinar

Learn More About Masterclasses, Courses, Books, Podcasts, Offers, *#ImpactLives* Membership, Career Mastermind Groups, Coaching, and the Career & Life Design Community!

CAREER AND LIFE
— MASTERY™ —

About the Author

Hassan Akmal is an American career and life mastery consultant, author, professor, thought leader, philanthropist, and former professional tennis player and athlete ambassador to the United States. He is best known for his Amazon best-selling book — *How to be a Career Mastermind* ™: *Discover 7 "YOU Matter" Lenses for a Life of Purpose, Impact, and Meaningful Work* and humanitarian work dedicated to Forced Migration and Health.

After over a decade as a senior leader in career services, he became the inaugural executive director of industry relations and career strategies at Columbia University in 2017 and founded the award-winning Career Design Lab. In 2018, he served on the National Association of Colleges and Employers (NACE) "Future of We" — Advisory Committee and served as a senior advisor to Graduway (now Gravyty), a prominent and top 10 global EdTech startup. He wrote the foreword for the book, *Career Revolution: A Design Thinking Approach to Career Development in a Post-Pandemic World*, authored by Graduway's CEO, Daniel Cohen. In April 2019, he delivered the keynote address on the "Future of Career Services" at the Global Leaders' Summit hosted at the University of California, Los Angeles (UCLA). He also serves on several other prominent boards internationally.

In December 2019, he was selected as a speaker for Columbia University's TEDx event that took place on March 27, 2021. His TEDx Talk entitled, "The Power to Design a Life You Love," was released in May 2021 and has received over 1.5 million views.

Prior to his current role, Akmal served as the executive director of the UCLA Career Center. There he led an ambitious re-imagination of career services. In September 2021, he became the Executive Director of Career and Professional Development at UC San Diego. His new book, published in May 2023, is entitled, *The Interior Design of Your Career and Life* ™. He also published a children's career and life design storybook entitled, *IMAGINE: You Are the Artist of Your Life*.

Hassan Akmal, M.B.A., M.P.H

Ameen

Made in the USA
Las Vegas, NV
08 May 2023